The *Resurgam* Submarine

'A Project for Annoying the Enemy'

Peter Holt

Archaeopress Archaeology

Archaeopress Publishing Ltd
Gordon House
276 Banbury Road
Oxford OX2 7ED

www.archaeopress.com

ISBN 978 1 78491 582 7
ISBN 978 1 78491 583 4 (e-Pdf)

© Archaeopress and Peter Holt 2017

Printed and bound in Great Britain by
Marston Book Services Ltd, Oxfordshire

All rights reserved. No part of this book may be reproduced, or transmitted, in any form or by any means, electronic, mechanical, photocopying or otherwise, without the prior written permission of the copyright owners.

This book is available direct from Archaeopress or from our website www.archaeopress.com

Contents

Acknowledgements vii
Introduction ix
Glossary xi
Timeline xiii
George William Littler Garrett 1
19th Century Submarines 3
Garrett and the Royal Navy 10
The *Egg* 13
Building *Resurgam* 16
    Introduction 16
    The Hull 17
    Wood Cladding 21
    Conning Tower and Fairing / Cutwater 21
    The Rudders and Hydroplanes 25
    The Lamm 'Fireless' Steam Engine 25
    The Engine 27
    Note: The Invention of the Snorkel 28
    Condenser 28
    The Blower 29
    Propeller 30
The *Resurgam* Submarine in Use 32
    Weight and Buoyancy 32
    Stability 35
    Life Support and the Pneumatophore 37
    Gas Calculations 37
    Environment 39
    Dynamics and Diving 40
The First and Last Voyage 44
Searching for *Resurgam* 49
    Pipe Route Survey 50
Rediscovery 52
The *SubMap* Project 55
    Introduction 55
        Phase 1 55
        Phase 2 55
        Phase 3 55
    SubMap Methods 57

    SubMap Geophysical Survey 59
    Operations 60
    Subsea Positioning 61
    Hull Position 63
    SubMap Wide Area Search 64
    Diver Search 65
    'Uri Geller' Targets 66
    SubMap Hull Recording 67
    SubMap Excavation 68
    Raising, Recording and Reburial 69
    3D Models 69
    SubMap Finds 71
    SubMap Corrosion Study 75
    SubMap Marine Biology Survey 76
    Discussion 80

Later Site History 81
    After SubMap 81
    2007 Wessex Archaeology Site Assessment 81
    After 2007 82

Site Formation 83
    Position A – 1880 to 1993 83
    Position B – 1993 to 1998 86
    Position C – 1998 to Present 88

Resurgam Today 91
    The Hull 91
    Conning Tower 94
    Fairing 96
    Timber Cladding 97
    Rudder and Hydroplanes 97
    Hull Interior 98
    Site 98

A Reanalysis of the Loss of *Resurgam* 100
    Why did Garrett report the submarine lost off Great Ormes Head, 20km away from where she sank? 100
    Did the *Elphin* ram the *Resurgam*, dent the conning tower and sink her? 101
    Was the conning tower hatch taken off deliberately? 101
    Why were all of the crew taken off the submarine when they knew the hatch could not be shut from the outside? 102
    How did the submarine sink? 102
    Fact and fiction 103

The End? 106

Appendix 1: Tables 109
    Table 1 - AUSS Targets from 1996 109
    Table 2: ADU Targets 03 Jun 1997 109
    Table 3: Corner Co-ordinates 110
    Table 4: Beacon positions 110
    Table 5: Control Point Positions 110
    Table 6: Metal detector targets 111
    Table 7: Uri Geller Targets 112

Appendix 2: The Open Letter 113
    An Open Letter to maritime archaeologists, shipwreck conservators, ICUCH/ICOMOS members, heritage practitioners, and stakeholders in *Resurgam*, about the endangered historic submarine *Resurgam* (1880) 113

References 115

List of Figures

Figure 1: George Garrett 1

Figure 2: Samuel Alstitt's submarine 5

Figure 3: Plan of the Ictineo II submarine and engine 7

Figure 4: Waddington's Porpoise 8

Figure 5: Garrett's prototype submarine as shown in the 1878 patent 13

Figure 6: The later design of the Egg based on a Cochran drawing 14

Figure 7: The Garrett Submarine Torpedo Boat from the Graphic magazine 17 January 1880 16

Figure 8: The plan of the Resurgam published in the journal The Engineer 18

Figure 9: An early sketch of the Resurgam only 30 ft long and reinforced with T section iron frames (RNSM) 19

Figure 10: A modified sketch of the submarine by Jack Aitkin showing the boiler arrangement, snorkel, engine and blower (RNSM) 19

Figure 11: The replica Resurgam at Woodside showing the faired shape of the cladding timbers. The original timbers were baulks 18 in thick rather than the smaller planks used on the replica built by AMARC trainees in 1997 20

Figure 12: Plan, Elevation and Section of Resurgam 22

Figure 13: Detail from a photograph of the submarine showing the conning tower hatch 23

Figure 14: Specification for construction noting the conning tower '1 Manhole screw inside and out' (RNSM) 24

Figure 15: Diagram of the propulsion system 26

Figure 16: Diagram of the propulsion system 29

Figure 17: Detail of a photograph of Resurgam showing the three-bladed propeller. The hull obscures the third blade. 30

Figure 18: Resurgam at Birkenhead just before launching, with Jackson (fwd), Price (aft) and Garrett holding his two year old daughter Georgina 44

Figure 19: Rhyl harbour in 1997 46

Figure 20: Chart showing the location of the wreck in relation to Rhyl and Great Ormes Head .. 47

Figure 21: Detail from the 1:5000 scale plan of the pipe route survey (Courtesy of Costain Ltd.) 50

Figure 22: Side scan sonar image of the submarine and associated scour (BHP Billiton) 51

Figure 23: Resurgam wreck site location off North Wales 53

Figure 24: Resurgam as she was seen in 1997 lying hard over on her starboard side, view from the bow towards the stern taken from ROV video footage 54

Figure 25: Detailed sketch of the submarine created during SubMap by Bill Turner 58

Figure 26: Terschelling moored over the top of the wreck during SubMap 59

Figure 27: Diver positioning a survey control point using the ROVTrak acoustic positioning system ... 62

Figure 28: Diver searching the seabed with an Aquascan pulse induction metal detector while being tracked by the ROVTrak acoustic positioning system 65

Figure 29: Plan of the site showing target locations on the seabed around the submarine 66

Figure 30: Fax from Geller showing his estimate for the location of the missing objects 66

Figure 31: Plan of the site showing the location of artefacts 67

Figure 32: West end of the trench showing the faired timber cladding and iron retaining straps 69

Figure 33: The beer can model of Resurgam 70

Figure 34: A 3D digital model of Resurgam created in 1997 70

Figure 35: Sketch of the site showing features referred to in the text (adapted from Gregory) ... 75

Figure 36: Site Plan for Position A with the hull upright and buried in the seabed 83

Figure 37: Three options for burial of the hull in the seabed 85

Figure 38: Site Plan for Position B showing movement of the hull from A to B 86

Figure 39: Proposed site formation sequence 87

Figure 40: Site Plan for Position C showing current position and attitude of the hull 88

Figure 41: Large diameter floating mooring rope attaching the ship to an anchor buoy in the distance 89

Figure 42: Plan sketch of the conning tower base 91

Figure 43: Video image of the two holes in the bow cone 93

Figure 44: The top of the forward hole in the bow cone showing plating pushed inwards 93

Figure 45: Sketch of the top of the conning tower from 1997 94

Figure 46: Photograph of Resurgam in 1997 from behind the conning tower looking forward. The scale cube in the large dent is 200 mm each side 95

Figure 47: Multibeam sonar image of Resurgam from 2011 (Bibby Hydromap Ltd.) 99

Figure 48: Plan showing the wreck location relative to Great Ormes Head and Rhyl 100

Figure 49: Resurgam lying nearly upright on the seabed in 2013 (Justin Owen) 106

Acknowledgements

Thanks go to the many people and organisations that have provided information for this book or have supported research and fieldwork on the *Resurgam* submarine. There have been many direct contributors to this book, most notably Alex Hildred, Nigel Boston and Stewart Wareing, with additional information from Simon Adey-Davies, Ian Cundy, Mark Newell, Mike Williams, Chris Holden, Dr Rohan Holt, the late Mike Bowyer and the late Martin Dean. Detailed technical advice about small submarines has been provided by Rob Shaw, Gary Gardner, Darren Orum, James Riggs and Paul Williams at MSubs Ltd. Many people read the drafts and suggested improvements but special thanks go to Mallory Haas and to Julie Williams for proof reading. Particular thanks go to William Garrett who spent a considerable amount of his own time and money searching for *Resurgam*; he helped record the wreck on the seabed during the SubMap Project and has since been an invaluable source of information.

Organisations and institutions that have supported this work include American Underwater Search and Survey Ltd., Arcre Archive Research, Bibby Hydromap Ltd., Boston Shipping Ltd., Bournemouth University, Cadw, Joint Nature Conservation Council, Liverpool Nautical Research Society, Marine Conservation Society, MSubs Ltd., the Nautical Archaeology Society, PP Electronics Ltd., Rhyl Yacht Club, The RN Submarine Museum, Sonardyne International Ltd. and Wessex Archaeology.

The SubMap Project survey and excavation team on *Terschelling* in 1997 were Alex Hildred (archaeological director), Nigel Boston (master of the *Terschelling*), Simon Adey-Davies, Paul Dart, Bill Garrett, Dr David Gregory, Jon Greenough, Dr Dick Hazelwood, Peter Holt, John Pitman and Greg Walker. The Archaeological Diving Unit team on SubMap (on *Xanadu*) were Martin Dean (project director), Mark Lawrence, Annabel Lawrence, Steve Liscoe and Ian Oxley. The NAS Survey contributors include G Adams, R Armstrong, Sue Barker, N Bolley, S Course, Ian Cundy, C Gidney, Sherrin Hibbard, C Jones, Doug McElvogue, T Millan, Garry Momber, Karen Moule, Ian Ross, N Taylor, R Toye, Bill Turner, J Williams and Robin Witheridge. The JNCC survey team were Rohan Holt, Paul Brazier, Paul Kay, Mark Inall, Peter Vaughan and Tim Brian, photographs were taken by R. Holt, P. Kay, and P. Brazier and video record was taken by T. Brian. Other help and contributions have kindly been given by the late Richard Bufton, Peter Campini, John Perry Fish, Fiona Gale, Mark Gorton, the late Keith Hurley, Cecil Jones, the late John Povah, Dr Mark Redknap and Sian Rees.

Introduction

What a marvellous adaptation of physics, pneumatics, and mechanics is displayed in a submarine, with which the highest standard of wholesale destruction is reached.[1]

For centuries inventors have been dreaming up schemes to allow people to submerge beneath the waves, stay a while then return again unharmed. Some of these inventors wished to discover what lay hidden in the depths or to recover sunken treasure, pearls or coral. Other inventors wanted to use the sea as a means to hide - to sneak up on an enemy, deliver a swift and fatal blow then escape unseen to safety. The *Resurgam* was intended for the latter task as she was primarily designed as a weapon of war. The title of this book comes from an Admiralty catalogue of inventions[2] that mentions the *Resurgam* under the category of '*Projects for Annoying the Enemy*'. The *Resurgam* submarine would more correctly be called a submersible as it is a vehicle that spends most of its time on the surface but has the capability to submerge, but as she is widely known as the *Resurgam* submarine we will keep it that way in this book. As with all submarines and submersibles, she is referred to as being a boat and not a ship.

The *Resurgam* submarine was the brainchild of an eccentric inventor that he realised in iron, timber, coal and steam. The inventor was George William Garrett, a curate from Manchester who designed and built the *Resurgam* submarine in 1879 using the limited technology available to a Victorian engineer on a small budget. This is not the story of Garrett himself; this story has already been told by William Scanlan-Murphy in his 1987 book *Father of the Submarine* and in Paul Bowers' book *The Garrett Enigma* published in 1999. Instead, this book tells the story of the submarine herself: how she was built, how she may have worked and what happened to her. The book briefly introduces Garrett the inventor then puts *Resurgam* in context by considering some other submarines being developed at the end of the 19th century. Garrett's relationship with his first prospective client, the Royal Navy, is related here as it is crucial to the story; it seems that Garrett was doomed to failure even if the submarine had worked because of Admiralty policy at that time. To experiment with some basic ideas Garrett built a tiny prototype submarine which suffered a number of re-designs and re-builds before she was set aside to make way for her larger and more warlike sister. We can gain some idea of how the *Resurgam* was constructed by reading surviving documents and plans; much of what we know about the *Resurgam* comes from an article that appeared in the 6th January 1882 edition of the journal *The Engineer* under the title *Garrett's Submarine Torpedo Boat*. The end of the tale tells how the *Resurgam* came to be lost in 1880, the truth is unknown but a version of the story can be pieced together from documents and newspaper reports. Unfortunately some aspects of the tale do not fit with what was found by archaeologists underwater so other ideas are explored at the end of the book. We have no reliable accounts of how well this submarine worked so modern analysis

---
[1] Ostler 1915
[2] National Archives, ADM 12/1023, 59-8

methods have been applied to calculate how well the *Resurgam* may have sailed, dived and kept her crew alive underwater.

This book includes first-hand experience of working underwater on the submarine in 1997, with details added from personal site notebooks, sketches, dive logs and discussions with divers who have been lucky enough to visit her. The *Resurgam* was the subject of Stewart Wareing's dissertation for his MA in Maritime Archaeology & History at the University of Bristol which he kindly made available for this book. Details and background information have been taken from books, journals and newspaper articles, papers in the National Archive and Royal Navy Submarine Museum archive, television programmes, web sites and PhD theses, all of which are listed in the references at the end.

Glossary

Term	Description
ACHWS	Advisory Committee on Historic Wreck Sites
ADU	Archaeological Diving Unit
APS	Acoustic Positioning System
AUSS	American Underwater Search and Survey Ltd
Awash	Of a submarine, running on the surface with her deck just submerged
Beam	The width of the hull
BSAC	British Sub-Aqua Club
Cadw	The Welsh Government's historic environment service
Closed up	With the submarines hatches closed, on the surface or underwater
Concretion	A hard mix of iron corrosion products, dead marine life and seabed material
Conning tower	A tall tower fitted on top of a submarine
Condenser	A condenser is used to condense steam back to water by cooling it
Cutwater	A hollow metal structure fitted on top of a submarine pressure hull
Displacement	The mass of water displaced by the submarine in water
DSV	Dive Support Vessel
Free flooding	A space that can flood with seawater when the submarine dives then drain once it has surfaced
GNSS	Global Navigation Satellite System, Global Positioning System, GPS
GPS	See GNSS
hp	Horsepower, a unit of power. 1 horsepower = 745.7 Watts
Hot well	A sump tank used to collect steam boiler condensate before recirculating it
Hydroplane	A horizontal rudder used to control the diving depth of the submarine

in	inch
Lap	The overlap between hull Strakes
LBL	Long BaseLine, a subsea positioning technique used by APS
NAS	Nautical Archaeology Society
Multibeam Echo Sounder (MBES)	A sonar instrument used to make very high resolution 3D images of the seabed
Pneumatophore	Self-contained breathing device designed and built by Garrett
Pressure hull	The part of the submarine's hull containing the machinery and crew
Receiver of Wreck, RoW	The authority responsible for management of items recovered from shipwrecks
RN	Royal Navy
RNSM	Royal Navy Submarine Museum
ROVTrak	A diver tracking system developed by Sonardyne International Ltd
Scour	An eroded depression in the seabed created by water currents flowing unevenly around an object
Silt	Light granular sediment less coarse than fine sand
Strake	A strip of hull material, in this case an iron plate
Trimmed down	Of a submarine; with all ballast tanks full of water and ready to dive
UT	Ultrasonic Thickness

Timeline

1852 July 4	George Garrett born
1864	Submarine *Hunley* sinks the *Housatonic*
1864	*Ictineo II* launched, possibly the first steam powered submarine
1878 May 8	Garrett files UK Patent No 1838, *Submarine Boats for Placing Torpedoes, etc.*
1879 March	Initial experiments carried out by Cochran & Co.
1879 April	Cochran and Co. awarded the contract to build *Resurgam*
1879 Nov 26	*Resurgam* lowered in to the Great Float in Birkenhead
1879 Dec 10	*Resurgam* leaves for Portsmouth
1879 Dec 12	*Resurgam* arrives at Rhyl
1880 Feb 24	*Resurgam* leaves Rhyl heading for Portsmouth
1880 Feb 25	*Resurgam* founders under tow
1880 May	Garrett demonstrates the pneumatophore in the river Seine
1882	Garrett struck from the clerical register
1882	Submarine *Nordenfelt 1* laid down near Stockholm, launched 1883
1898 Dec	French submarine *Gustave Zédé* successfully attacks a battleship with torpedoes
1900	British Admiralty commissions a series of experiments into anti-submarine warfare
1900 April	*Holland VI* purchased by the US Government
1900 Dec	British Admiralty contract Vickers to build first submarines for the Royal Navy
1902 Feb 26	George Garrett dies
1925	Engineer George Price tells the story of how *Resurgam* was lost
1975	First search for Resurgam, by the Oxford Laboratory for Archaeology
1981	Royal Navy search
1983	Royal Navy Submarine Museum search
1985	George W. Garrett transfers title of the submarine to the RN Submarine Museum
1987	Marine Archaeological Survey search
1989	William Garrett and Richard Bufton search
1992	William Garrett search
1993	William Garrett search
1993	Douglas to Point of Ayr gas pipe installed
1993-95	*Resurgam pulled from the seabed?*
1995 Oct	*Resurgam* located
1996 April	ADU visit to the site with the finder
1996 June	Emergency designation under the Protection of Wrecks Act (1973)
1996 June	Garrett survey with AUSS, ADU visits *Resurgam* with *Terschelling*
1996	Sport divers remove objects from the wreck
1996	Resurgam Committee set up by the RN Submarine Museum
1997 June	SubMap Project (4th -15th)
1998	ADU visit

1998	*Submarine hull is moved*
1998	Resurgam Trust set up
1999 April	ADU visit, confirmed that the submarine had moved
1999 June	Bowyer visits site with Police divers
2000	ADU visit
2001	ADU visit with ROV inspection
2006 July	Missing porthole is handed to the Receiver of Wreck then passed on to the RNSM
2006 Sept	Wessex Archaeology site assessment
2007	BSAC Trafford undertake conservation work on the site
2012	BSAC Chester undertake conservation work on the site

George William Littler Garrett

George William Littler Garrett was born in Lambeth in London on the 4th of July 1852, the third son of John and Georgina Garrett; his father was curate of the local St Mary's Church. In 1857 his father took up a position in Penzance in Cornwall at St Paul's church which overlooks Mounts Bay, and it is in this nautical environment that young George Garrett may have first become interested in the sea. The move to Cornwall was due in part to the interest John's patron had in his work which may have come to the attention of Albert, the Prince Consort, through their Masonic ties. As noted by Murphy 'the *family talent for currying favour with the influential was only matched by a woeful inability to manage money*'. Much of Garrett's life would be affected by his father's financial troubles and George himself would die almost destitute in New York after a period serving with the US Army Engineers during the Spanish-American War.

Figure 1: George Garrett

The financial difficulties began in July 1861 after John Garrett agreed to take over a post in Christ Church, in Moss Side near Manchester after the death of his patron. The previous incumbent had exaggerated the income of the parish and what little John Garrett had to live on was spent on the upkeep of the *'decrepit jerry-built pile of used bricks'* that was his church and the rent for the imposing Greenheys Hall which he chose as his rectory. Despite the problems with the Parish, George was able to board at Rossall School where he showed an interest and aptitude for the sciences. George was withdrawn to the local Manchester Grammar School after his father became embroiled in an embezzlement charge; although found innocent, Garrett Senior was left with fines of £2,500 and could no longer afford the school fees.

George left the Grammar school in 1869 and spent nine months teaching in Seighford village school in Staffordshire, before enrolling as a 'Pensioner' student at the University of Dublin (Figure 1). During this period Garrett took evening lessons in chemistry with Professor Henry Roscoe at Owen's College, taking a particular interest in the chemistry of respiration and breathing in confined spaces. By 1872 Garrett had begun research into human respiration while working at the Kensington Museum and the results of this work would later allow him to design a self-contained breathing apparatus crucial to the development of *Resurgam*. After meeting his future wife, Jane Parker, while working at Pocock College in Cambridge, Garrett was then able to study at Trinity College with help from his fiancée's parents, graduating in 1875 with an Honours degree in Experimental Sciences. Once he had graduated, George was requested by his father to become the curate in his parish as he was struggling by himself. Instead, Garrett chose to spend a year in Fiji and New Zealand *'teaching and practising navigation in all its branches'* before returning to England the following year where he was ordained as deacon at the age of 25.

The Russia-Turkish war began shortly after George's appointment in May 1877. Garrett read reports of the Russian Navy being repelled by Turkish anti-torpedo boat defences, simply a row of small vessels linked by rope, and he saw the need for a vessel that could submerge and slip under these floating barriers. It was this event that sparked his interest in submarine boats and led Garrett to develop the *Resurgam* submarine.

19th Century Submarines

Man has been exploring the sea for thousands of years both on and beneath the waves with varying degrees of success and varying levels of peril for the explorers themselves. By the 19th Century, underwater exploration was still done at a distance, investigating the sea by probing it remotely from the surface or by making brief excursions in person. Yet scientists and engineers wanted to explore the sea from within and for much longer. At that time diving apparatus was being developed that allowed a man to visit the seabed for a short time but the time underwater was limited by the supply of air available or the problems of decompression sickness. Some wanted to explore the sea to investigate what lived there, some wanted to recover its riches in the form of pearls and sunken treasure while others wished to use it for warfare. The surface of the sea hides anything beneath it very effectively so an underwater vessel or 'submarine boat' could be used to approach enemy ships unseen, disable them with mines then creep away to safety. By the 1870s the submarine boat was part of British popular culture, partly due to Jules Verne and his book *20000 Leagues under the Sea* published at the beginning of the decade, and also because the national newspapers were announcing the latest submarine developments alongside scaremongering articles about the threat they posed to national security. Warfare was the main driving force behind most early submarine developments and it was the motivation behind Garrett's decision to design and build *Resurgam* since he intended to sell his submarines to the British Royal Navy.

The development of a successful submarine in the late 19th century would irreversibly change the balance of power at sea, so these inventions could be considered to be the 'weapons of mass destruction' of their time. Any port that was guarded by submarines was safe as it would be too risky for surface ships to attack against an unseen and undetectable enemy that was carrying torpedoes. A submarine fitted with a spar torpedo on its nose was sneaky but it still retained some of the 'whites of their eyes' style of close-quarters naval combat that had been the gentlemanly option so far. The spar torpedo submarine had to get very close to the enemy ship it was attacking as the torpedo had to be physically pushed on to the hull. The development of the self-propelled 'locomotive' torpedo changed all that; a submarine underwater could creep towards the enemy ship, fire off a torpedo at a distance then skulk away unseen. No wonder the Royal Navy thought this was an underhand and un-gentlemanly form of combat; if their proud battleships were to be destroyed they would prefer it to be done by gallant enemy officers commanding smart ships and wearing clean uniforms, not by some anonymous mechanic in dirty overalls driving a submarine.

Designing a submarine is difficult as there are many interconnected factors to consider. Making a submarine submerge beneath the waves is relatively simple; the difficulty lies in making it return to the surface when required and with the crew still alive and well. To build a submarine requires a detailed knowledge of naval architecture, mechanics, buoyancy, stability, propulsion systems and life support.

Failure to comprehend any one of those critical factors and the submarine would not work and could result in the loss of life; there was a huge amount at stake but there were also huge rewards for anyone who succeeded.

By the time Garrett was doing his research into how to build a submarine there was already a small body of knowledge about how it should be done. More accurately, there were many examples of how it should not be done as most of the attempts to build a submarine had ended in failure, and quite often involved the loss of the submarine and the submarine's crew. Finding out about any new designs was difficult as details about submarines built for warfare were often well-guarded secrets. Inventors kept their inventions to themselves and only shared their ideas with select governments; their work could be offered to a friendly nation, a foe or often both at the same time, the only stipulation was that someone had to pay handsomely for what was on offer. These inventions were not well advertised, any plans and documents were rarely published and these devices were also subject to hype and exaggeration by their inventors and promoters. Tidbits of information about submarine boats could be gleaned by spies so they could be sold on, yet the inventors themselves would pass on misinformation to deliberately thwart their competitors. This lack of reliable information on this subject still causes problems today. It would be impossible to work out the actual sequence of 19th century submarine developments as many books on the subject mention a selection of submarines but none of the books are comprehensive. For example, Pesce's lengthy and beautifully illustrated book *La Navigation Sous-Marine* describes hundreds of submarines from the earliest attempts until 1906, yet it omits to mention Monturiol and his technically advanced *Ictineo II*. But Pesce does include D'Allest and his petrol-powered submarine from 1885 which rarely gets a mention anywhere else. It is impossible to say what Garrett knew about other submarine designs in 1878 when he was putting his plans together. It is likely that the inventor would have had access to the journal *The Engineer* which provided quality information about recent engineering developments or the results of any published trials. It is also likely that Garrett had read one of the few books on the subject, Barnes' *Submarine Warfare* published in 1869 and he may have read Barber's 1875 *Lecture on Submarine Boats and Their Application to Torpedo Operations* through his contacts in the Admiralty. What else Garrett had read or learned we cannot know, but his two submarines show that he was aware of the critical design issues of weight and buoyancy, stability, motive power and life support.

Garrett knew that his submarine had to include a mechanical propulsion system. Many man-powered designs had already been built and all had demonstrated that human power was not viable, as you simply could not put enough people inside a submarine to make an effective propulsion system. The options for mechanical power were few at that time so only included chemical heat engines, rudimentary electrical motors, compressed air engines and steam power as petrol and diesel engines chosen for later designs had yet to be developed. Garrett chose to use steam propulsion from this limited list of options, probably because it was the most reliable and available at that time. One of the earliest proposals for a steam powered submarine came from M. Armand-Maziere in 1795 who submitted to the French Committee of Public Safety a set of plans for a submarine vessel which was to be propelled by oars actuated by a steam engine.

This device was intended to gain the upper hand for France in the Revolutionary wars against England as it was a potential means of defeating the might of the Royal Navy. This design used oars to propel the submarine and included separate oars that were used to submerge it; these were the prototypes for vertical thrusters that were re-invented again a century later for use on submarines.

The paucity of information about submarine developments and the slow rate at which it was disseminated produced curious side-effects. Many submarine inventors failed, fell by the wayside and were never heard of again, yet their unpublished designs incorporated radical new features that had to be re-invented later on. A good example of this is the periscope as it was a design that emerged separately on a number of different occasions. The French submarine *Gymnote* was fitted with a periscope in 1880 and the Spanish *Peral* had one in 1888. Simon Lake, another successful early submarine designer, is often credited with the invention of the periscope because in 1902 he produced his 'omniscope'. In 1900, an unknown naval officer called Bacon became the first Inspecting Captain of Submarine Boats for the Royal Navy and was charged with commissioning the Holland submarines that had recently been ordered by the Admiralty. Bacon didn't think much of the design sent over from America so set about designing the first workable submarines for the Royal Navy which eventually became the original 'A' class. During this process he hit upon the idea of the periscope, as the original Holland design didn't have one, and claimed invention of the device years later in his autobiography as he was unaware of its prior use in the submarines *Gymnote* and *Peral*.

For an example of an early submarine design that was forgotten you need look no further than Samuel Alstitt from Mobile in Alabama, who in 1863 built a 21 m long submarine as a stealth weapon for use during the American civil war (Figure 2). The submarine was novel in many ways, not least its propulsion system that used steam power on the surface and electricity when submerged, the first recorded use of a mixed propulsion system in a submarine. Alstitt's design included ballast tanks to enable the vessel to submerge; it retained a reserve of buoyancy so the boat had to be driven under the surface but could be held at depth using its bow hydroplanes. The limited air supply in the boat was renewed from compressed air cylinders in the bows. Later authors noted that this vessel failed because of its propulsion system as the electric motors were not powerful enough and the very early batteries gave off poisonous fumes when discharged at a high current.

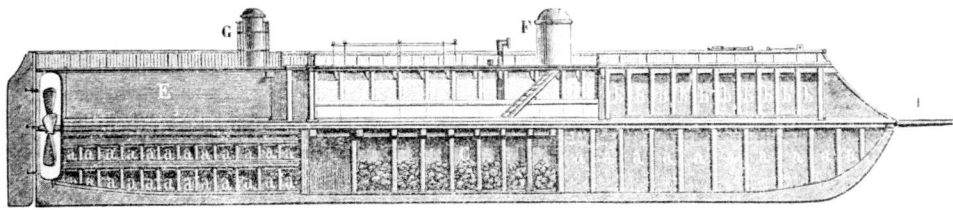

Figure 2: Samuel Alstitt's submarine

The French *Plongeur* (*Diver*) designed by Siméon Bourgeois and launched in 1863 is often quoted as being the first mechanically propelled submarine. The *Plongeur* had an 80hp compressed air engine powered by gas delivered at 180 psi (12 bar) from 23 copper air tanks which took up so much space that the boat had to be 44.5 m long. This submarine was also notable for being the first to be fitted with a lifeboat on the back deck. The extremely long and thin submarine was longitudinally unstable so it was impossible to steer; it was tested occasionally until 1872 before being converted into a water tanker.

The *Ictineo II* was a submarine designed and built by Narcís Monturiol, a Spanish intellectual, radical, artist and engineer. Unusually for a submarine designer at this time, Monturiol was passionate about doing works for the public good and he hoped that the development of a submarine would lead to the 'liberation of human kind'. The reason to create a submarine was to explore the depths of the sea and to harvest coral from the seabed. Monturiol first built a 7 m long prototype submarine called *Ictineo I*; this led to the development of a larger 17 m long boat built from 100 mm thick olivewood sheathed in copper sheet 2 mm thick. Monturiol calculated that the 72 ton fish-shaped hull reinforced by oak rings could withstand pressure at 500 m, but set the working depth to 50 m just to be on the safe side (Figure 3). The *Ictineo II* was man-powered when it was first built and required 20 men inside the hull to operate a crankshaft which drove the single propeller. This sophisticated submarine was fitted with main ballast tanks that were used to submerge and smaller trim tanks used to compensate for the loss of buoyancy caused by the compression of the hull at depth. The boat was fitted with two independent sets of weights which could be dropped to gain buoyancy in an emergency. *Ictineo II* had a life support system including oxygen generation and carbon dioxide (CO_2) removal, a means of removing bacteria from the air and even a way of dealing with '*gases created by poor digestion*'. The boat was fitted with 19 large portholes so the crew could see the wonders of the deep, lit by a very bright underwater light powered by burning hydrogen and oxygen gases. *Ictineo II* was launched at Barcelona in Spain on 2nd October 1864 and she completed her first sea trials on 20th May the following year, diving to a maximum depth of 30 m. Experiments with the vessel on more than 60 dives included sealing up the crew for 8 hours to note the effect on their health and testing an anti-ship gun that could be fired from underwater. The main problem with the *Ictineo II* was that it could only achieve 1 to 2 knots under human power. Monturiol thought this was not fast enough to counter subsea currents so he refused to employ the vessel to harvest coral to earn money to pay for further development work. In an attempt to gain more speed, Monturiol converted a small steam engine so that it could be fitted in the submarine with the necessary heat to produce steam coming from an exothermic chemical reaction rather than a conventional furnace. As a neat side-effect the chemical reaction also generated oxygen that the crew could breathe.

The new engine provided the additional thrust required and on 22nd October 1867 the submarine completed a 16km surface run at 3.5 knots. A static underwater test alongside the dock in December showed that the basic principle of the engine worked, but one huge problem remained. The chemical engine quickly made the inside of the submarine unbearably hot, rising to 50° C in just 20 minutes, so the submarine could only be dived briefly a few metres below the surface before the crew had to return to

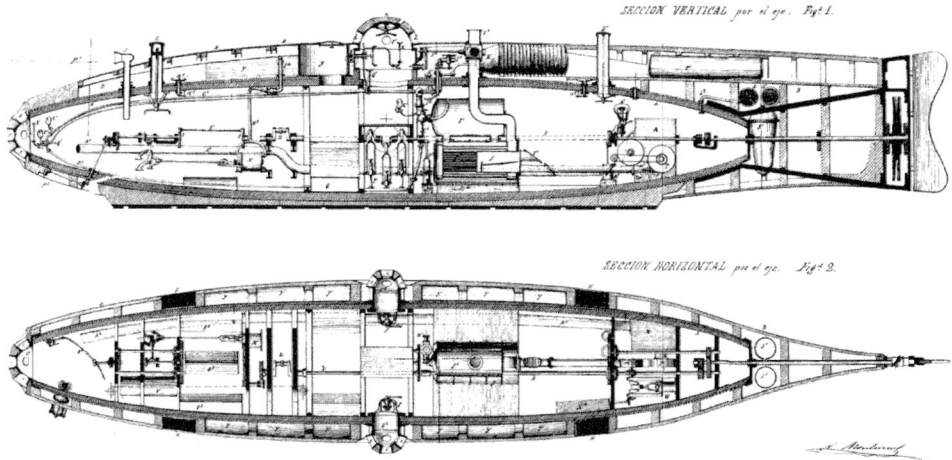

Figure 3: Plan of the Ictineo II submarine and engine

the surface to cool off. The wooden hull was a good insulator and retained all the heat generated from within. More work needed to be done to design and build a cooling system that would allow the submarine to be used but this in turn would require more funding. Monturiol had already spent 100,000 Duros building the submarine; this was a huge sum of money and at that time was enough to purchase several frigates or 160kg of gold. But after 12 long years of development the submarine still could not be used to recover coral that could be sold to recoup some of the exorbitant costs. Finally, on 23rd December 1867 the company formed to build the new submarine ran out of money, the shipyard where she was built took the submarine in lieu of payment and on 21st February 1868 this engineering marvel was broken up for scrap. It seems that *Ictineo II* only completed static dives alongside the dock with her steam engine fitted and never did propel herself underwater under power, so perhaps she was not the first steam powered submarine after all?

James Franklin Waddington was another submarine designer working in Birkenhead at the same time as Garrett. Waddington succeeded J. Aitkin as chief draughtsman for Cochran & Co., the company which built the *Resurgam* submarine, shortly after the *Resurgam* had been completed. Waddington then went into business for himself, setting up a yard in Seacombe just over the Great Float dock to the north of Birkenhead. In 1886 Waddington built an electric powered submarine called the *Porpoise*; she was spindle shaped, 11 m (37 ft) long and 2 m (6 ft) diameter, divided into three compartments with space in the centre compartment for the crew of two (Figure 4). The central compartment contained all the machinery and had ballast tanks fitted in the bottom while the bow and stern cones contained compressed air. The *Porpoise* was powered by an 8 hp electric motor driven by 45 batteries that it was reported could move the submarine at 8 knots for 8 hours; she was not the first electric submarine but she was certainly one of the first of this type to work successfully. This submarine was fitted with a number of devices that allowed her to dive. Ballast tanks around the keel of the

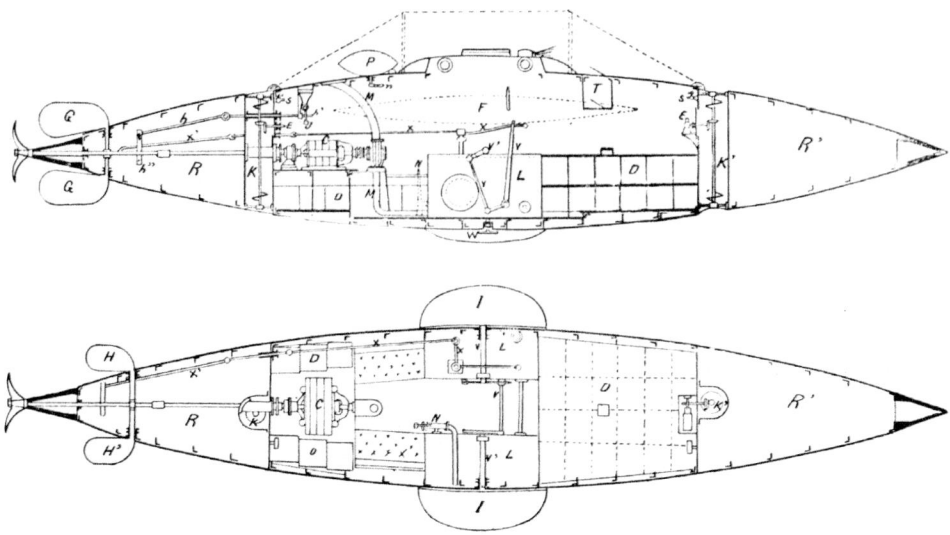

Figure 4: Waddington's Porpoise

vessel in the central section provided a large amount of positive buoyancy when the submarine was afloat on the surface with her tanks empty. To dive, the ballast tanks would be flooded leaving a small amount of reserve buoyancy which could be overcome by two vertically mounted tunnel thrusters, one in the bow and one in the stern.

The *Porpoise* also had two hydroplanes mounted in the centre of the hull; these were designed to maintain the boat on an even keel automatically as they were actuated by an electric motor controlled by a pendulum. If the pendulum detected a change in the pitch of the vessel the motor would automatically tilt the hydroplanes in the correct direction to level the hull. In the event of a serious problem the boat was fitted with a large keel weight that could be jettisoned allowing the submarine to float back to the surface. Armament for the boat included two Whitehead locomotive torpedoes mounted on the outside of the hull and an electrically-detonated floating mine torpedo attached behind the conning tower which when released would attach itself to the hull of an enemy vessel before being exploded remotely. The *Porpoise* performed well in sea trials during March and April 1886 but despite being seen by representatives from the navies of a number of countries, the demonstrations did not result in any contracts and Waddington went bankrupt in 1887. The *Porpoise* was anchored for nearly two years just below the high water mark opposite Marine Terrace in Wallasey before she was broken up for scrap.

The man most usually credited with the development of the modern submarine was John Holland, an Irishman born in 1841 who emigrated to the United States in 1873. Holland's first submarine, called *Holland 1,* was a tiny boat weighing 2¼ tons into which a single person fitted rather snugly. This prototype was launched on 22 May 1878 and it was proved to work successfully after the usual teething problems had been dealt with. This boat retained a small amount of positive buoyancy when dived and used hydroplanes in the middle of the hull to force it under the water when underway. *Holland 1* was fitted with an early internal combustion engine designed by George Brayton. During sea trials the engine steadfastly refused to work when powered by petrol so the resourceful Holland hooked it up using a long rubber hose to a steam boiler on the support vessel above and powered the engine remotely. On 6th June that year the submarine was demonstrated to the Irish backers of his project who were representatives of the Fenian Skirmishing Fund. With the proof of concept proved, Holland removed the engine and scuttled the little boat under a bridge, where it was partly dismantled by salvors looking for scrap before being raised and recovered some years later. Holland subsequently noted that the mid-position hydroplanes were cumbersome as they retarded forward motion and required too much power to drive underwater. Work began on Holland's second submarine in May 1879 and it was launched in May 1881. This 31 ft long, 19 ton boat was powered by a 15 to 17hp two cylinder modified Brayton engine which could push the boat along at 9 knots. Based on the experience with his prototype Holland decided to mount the hydroplanes aft by the propeller on this new design. The second Holland boat became known as the *Fenian Ram*; it was tested in June 1881 and was the most successful of the early submarines.

This was the beginning of the end for the backyard submarine engineers. Once a working submarine had been demonstrated by Holland the development of submarines was taken out of the hands of independent inventors and given to teams of naval architects working in the arms industry.

Garrett and the Royal Navy

The Royal Navy at the turn of the century was firmly of the opinion that fleets of huge battleships were the way to protect England's shores. Victorian battleships were impressive, ostentatious and expensive weapons of war that were commanded by gentlemen in impeccable uniforms standing on spotless wooden decks and surrounded by shining brightwork. These were not just weapons of war, they were a proud statement about the might of the British Empire, and were maintained in such strength and quantity to ensure that no other surface fleet from a foreign power could threaten them. The situation changed dramatically in 1864 when the 1240 ton United States steam sloop-of-war *Housatonic* was sunk by the tiny submarine *Hunley*, the first submarine to sink a warship. Despite being as lethal to her crew as she was to the enemy, the *Hunley* proved that battleships were vulnerable to attack from below. With a little more development the world would see submarines progress from being inventors' madcap ideas to viable weapons of war. Soon the big battleships would be defenceless against an enemy hidden beneath the waves, especially one that could strike at a distance using one of Whitehead's new locomotive torpedoes.

A successful submarine design would change the balance of power at sea instantly and perhaps, irrevocably. Britain had the most to lose if submarines ever became useful as the defence of the realm relied on some very large and very expensive battleships which were beyond the means of most nations. The submarine was a cheap and easily produced weapon which was affordable for almost any nation however small. At a stroke, instead of having to concern itself with threats from just one or two rich countries, Britain now had to worry about all of them. The battleship had kept the peace at sea for many years just as the nuclear deterrent has suppressed major global conflicts in modern times. So the effect of the arrival of the submarine in the late 19th century would be similar to a nation today finding a way to disarm their enemy's entire nuclear weapons arsenal. There was now a significant reason for the battleship-obsessed Royal Navy to be worried. The position the Navy took was to be dismissive in public about these new tin-pot submarines, a policy that was deliberately intended to suppress the development of submarine boats. What the Admiralty did not do was ignore them; in fact they had recorded information about more than 320 19th century submarine prototypes and investigated a dozen in detail.

It was at this time that Garrett appeared on the scene and he became just one of many engineers who were offering submarines to the Royal Navy. Some of the hopeful inventors are listed in Admiralty document 59-8; the document is a catalogue of correspondence that mentions Garrett and the *Resurgam* under the category of '*Projects for Annoying the Enemy*'. The few pages of the catalogue either side of where the *Resurgam* is mentioned provide a tiny window into the world of Victorian inventors keen to make their fortune. Letters containing ideas for the defence of ships against torpedoes are well represented as are new torpedo designs and proposals for novel submarines, with a scattering of very strange ideas to add a little colour. Wading through all the correspondence must have kept a team of assessors busy sorting the wheat from an extensive range of chaff. Reading through the catalogue we find that Mr Poole's design for a submarine was declined by the Navy as were the plans submitted by a Lt. Atkinson and a Mr J. Cochrane. Mr Rogers must have corresponded earlier as he wrote later with improvements in his plans for a submarine boat. Mr Jones only sent a model of a submarine so he was asked by the Admiralty to make a real one; a later letter said that this would cost them £18,800 so his plans were declined. The Whitehead torpedo was well established by this time yet the list includes many torpedo designs from the likes of Messrs Knapp, Liardet, Cook and Hall. Some rejected inventors took the time to write back in a huff, with a Mr Leonard pointing out that '*he will dispose of his secret in other quarters*' as the comment from the Navy on his brainchild was '*plans submitted, useless, declined*'. Some of the more interesting and unusual submissions included a design from Mr Holt (no relation) for 'a balloon for destroying ships' and MacDonald's 'rocket torpedo', while Mr Bohn and Mr Smith both offered a pamphlet on 'Greek fire torpedo boats'. The last two sound more hazardous to the operator than to the enemy. Mr Woolly suggested '*India rubber be added to ships below the waterline for defence against torpedoes*', but it had been carefully noted in the list that that a prior claim to this idea had been made by a Mr Walker. But top of the grandiose plans was from Mr Carter who submitted an idea for '*a means of destroying a whole fleet*'; this was clearly a man who could never be accused of aiming too low.

Garrett made several trips to Portsmouth in 1878 and 1879 in his bid to interest the Admiralty in his designs. He consulted with naval officials through an intermediary called Hugh Birley, a colleague of Garrett who also knew the First Lord and the Secretary of the Admiralty socially.

In December 1878 Garrett made an offer to the Navy '*to build submarine vessels with the power to remain under water for a certain fixed time on condition that the Admiralty purchase it if successful for £10,000* '. But underneath is simply written 'Cannot accept'.

Despite declining the offer the Admiralty still expressed an interest in seeing a demonstration of Garrett's invention, maintaining the policy of keeping a wary eye on developments in the field, but that is probably as far as the relationship went. Garrett was head and shoulders above the competition at that time and his submarine design was noticed by the Admiralty. Writing later in 1901 in a memorandum on the subject of Submarine Boats, Rear-Admiral Wilson, Third Sea Lord and Controller of the Navy, stated that "*a very well thought-out design for a submarine boat was brought to my attention while commander of the* Vernon *about 1879, which only required only one small addition which any Torpedo Officer could have supplied to make it efficient*"; clearly a reference to the *Resurgam*.

Documentary evidence suggests that Garrett built *Resurgam* at his own expense and it was unlikely that the Admiralty would have contracted Garrett to build and demonstrate his submarine as that was not their policy. However, Garrett asked the Admiralty to refund his costs after the loss of *Resurgam*. Needless to say the Admiralty denied any responsibility and a correspondence took place "*relative to trials by Admiralty officers and alleged encouragement to Mr Garrett to build the boat*", with the outcome that the Admiralty refused to pay up.

The quotes in the Rhyl Journal that Garrett had been offered £60,000 by the Admiralty and £144,000 by the Russian government for *Resurgam* was clearly Garrett hype , as the Holland submarines built for the Royal Navy a few years later in 1903 cost just £35,000 each.

The decision by the Admiralty to investigate submarines while simultaneously holding back their progress was successful for quite some time. In the same memo that noted *Resurgam*, Rear-Admiral Wilson said; *'Each design has been carefully examined and sufficient experiment has been made in each case to ascertain its probable value. It has then been quietly dropped with the result of delaying the development of the submarine boat for about 20 years.'*

But In December 1898, news was received at the Admiralty that the French submarine *Gustave Zédé* had successfully attacked a French battleship with dummy torpedoes. The French were the first to incorporate submarines into their front line Navy and at this time led the world in development of the submarine as a practical weapon. In April 1900, with this looming menace now present in the French and other navies, the Admiralty quietly commissioned a series of experiments into anti-submarine warfare. The main difficulty with this proposal was that the Navy had no real experience with submarines and had no idea what to defend against, so a proposal was put forward by Wilson to purchase a submarine for trials.

This led to the purchase of the Holland type submarines built by Vickers and the formation of the Royal Navy submarine service.

The *Egg*

Having been inspired by events in the Russia-Turkish war Garrett got on with designing his first submarine which was intended to be a small prototype to be used for evaluating design ideas. On the 8th May 1878 Garrett patented a '*Submarine Boat for Placing Torpedoes, &c*' with this description:

> '*I generally construct the vessel of small dimensions, a handy size being about 14 feet long (when arranged to contain only one man), so as to be easily lifted by the davits of an ironclad or other ship, or from a pier or other structure.*'

The design of the prototype was modified between the time of publication of the patent and its construction by Cochran & Co. in Duke Street, Birkenhead. Cochran & Co. had been started in 1878 by James Taylor Cochran and Edward Compton as a general engineering and shipbuilding works but later became famous for the Cochran boiler, a compact and efficient vertical design that could be used to provide portable steam power.

Garrett's prototype submarine was not given a name, it is often referred to as the *Curate's Egg*, or just the *Egg*, and sometimes incorrectly called *Resurgam I*. The *Egg* was 14 ft (4.3 m) long, 5 ft (1.5 m) in diameter and weighed just 4.5 tons.

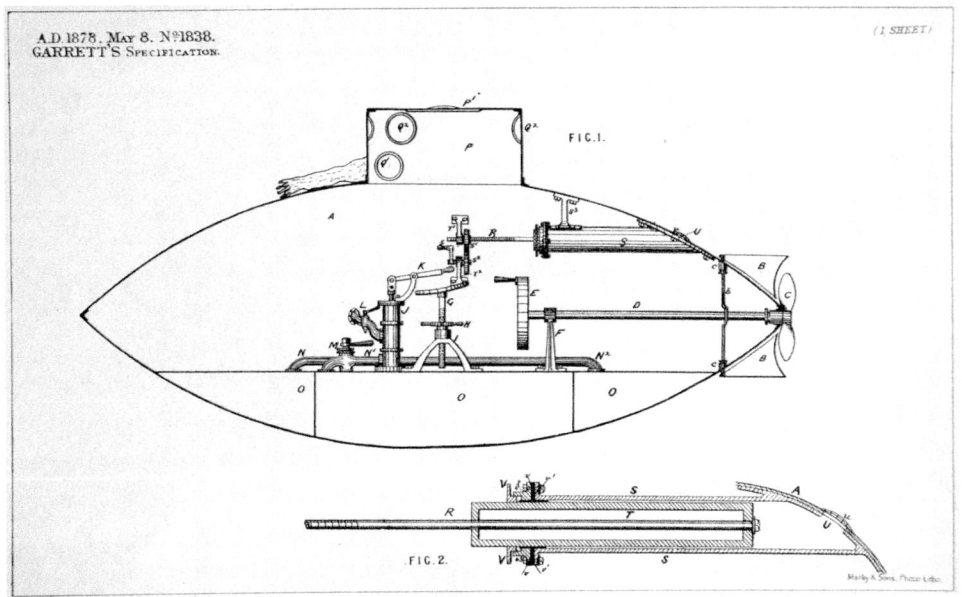

Figure 5: Garrett's prototype submarine as shown in the 1878 patent

The initial design had a hand-cranked propeller for propulsion with stern hydroplanes for diving and a rudder for steering (Figure 5). The boat included ballast tanks mounted low down in the hull and a piston mechanism that was used to vary the submarine's displacement so the boat would submerge. To dive, the ballast tanks were filled until the boat had sunk down to diving trim, the piston would be withdrawn inside the hull to decrease displacement, this would reduce buoyancy and the submarine would sink beneath the surface. To rise, the same piston was pushed out, displacement would be increased and the submarine would surface; the ballast tanks could then be emptied and the *Egg* would be afloat. The later design for the boat omitted the piston mechanism, most likely as it was not effective and took up too much room inside the tiny hull. This invention also included watertight sleeves fitted to the conning tower so the submariner could poke his arms out of the hull and attach mines to the hulls of enemy ships. A later modification used foot treadles to drive the propeller leaving the crew's hands free to operate the controls, as shown in Figure 6. This version omitted the piston mechanism so relied on just the ballast tanks to submerge. Trials of the prototype in a dock called the East Float were reported in the Liverpool Weekly Mercury in 1916 and wrongly attributed to the later and larger *Resurgam*:

> 'Her favourite run was from the grain warehouses to the entrance to the Egerton Dock. Her movements were slow, and how she was propelled I cannot say, but on her trials I saw her being submerged. By the ripples made on the surface you could always tell where she was, and now and then you could see her diver-shaped helmet come to the surface. I suppose that was to fix her position.'

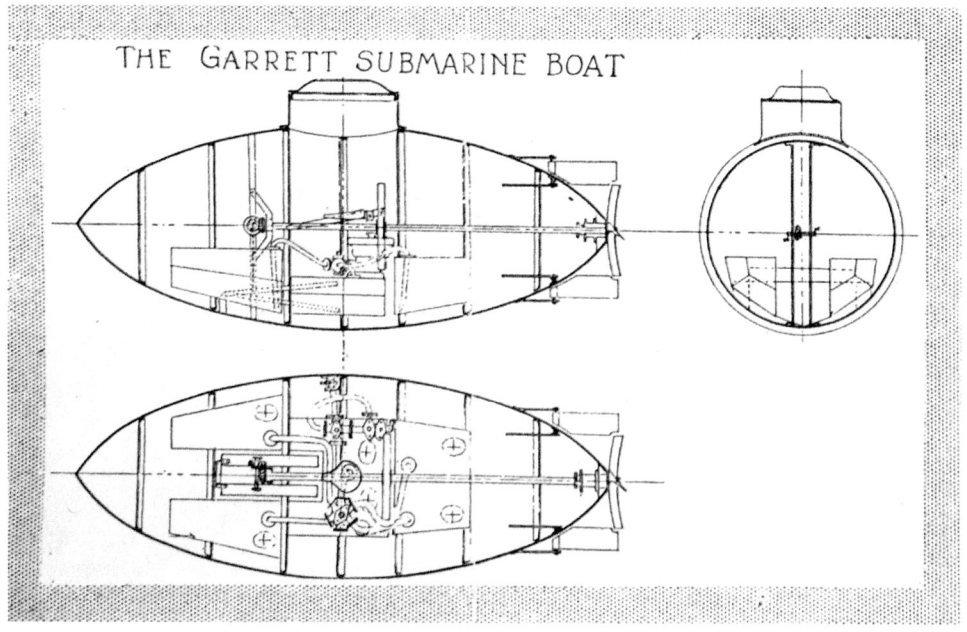

Figure 6: The later design of the Egg based on a Cochran drawing

The *Egg* was a working model with a short operating life. Its fate is not known but an article in the magazine Sea Breezes suggests that the *Egg* ended up in the yard of the other submarine designer Mr. Waddington at Seacombe just north of Birkenhead, a tale told to the article author by an old tugboat man some years after the events. This may be a tale confused with another as Waddington's own *Porpoise* submarine was anchored off Seacombe for some years before being broken up.

Building *Resurgam*

Introduction

The curate's first attempt at making a submarine gave him the confidence to build something more adventurous and Garrett's second attempt would take full advantage of Cochran & Co's boilermaking abilities. Garrett wrote to the engineering company on the 31st March 1879 requesting an estimate on a set of new specifications with the caveat '*I do not want the immediate price to be such as will frighten, and perhaps stop the proper carrying out of my plans*'. It seems that his plans may have included a visit to the Admiralty, as in the same letter he noted that he would be in Portmouth all of that week; he was clearly convinced that his next vessel would be of interest to the Royal Navy.

Garrett visited the Cochran & Co. in April to clarify his plans for a new and larger submarine to be called *Resurgam* (Latin for 'I will rise again') and a draughtsman began to transfer the idea into reality (Figure 7). The vessel was constructed over the next five months with the bill for the new vessel coming to £1,538; if this frightened Garrett or not we will never know but it did not stop his plans.

The archive of the Royal Navy Submarine Museum (RNSM) holds in its collections a series of correspondence between Garrett and the engineering company Cochran & Co. which built *Resurgam*.

Using a combination of Garrett's own designs, the modifications made by Cochran & Co, the 1882 drawing in *The Engineer* (Figure 8) and the dimensions produced by archaeological surveys we can estimate how *Resurgam* took shape and in what form she left the Birkenhead plant. On the 31st March 1879 Garrett sent a letter and sketch of what he envisaged the *Resurgam* to look like. The sketch in Figure 9 shows

Figure 7: The Garrett Submarine Torpedo Boat from the Graphic magazine 17 January 1880

a vessel of only 30 ft (9.14 m), each section equally divided into 3 parts requiring six 1 inch (25.4 mm) thick iron plates of varying widths, for the cone ends 4 ft (1.21 m) and for the middle section 5 ft (1.52 m). In the letter he asked for a vessel *'40 ft. long and 7 feet in diameter with 20 ft cylinder and two 10 ft points'*.

Garrett noted that he would like the vessel to be built to this scale as he was satisfied that the proportions were fit for its intended purpose. Garrett's ideas would be translated by Jack Aitken, draughtsman at Cochran & Co., after a meeting on the 7th April where Garrett met with the company and his ideas were discussed.

A letter dated on the 10th of that month details how *Resurgam* should be constructed. A later plan of the *Resurgam* held in the archive is attributed to either Garrett or Aitken and this plan shows the layout of the sub-systems and their position; the boiler and blower are in place and the inlet pipe is identifiable in the fairing (Figure 10). The design was quite literally drawn on the back of an envelope so it may not accurately reflect the design of the submarine that was constructed. This submarine was the first of a design never previously built and any problems encountered during construction will have been solved as they went along, most probably without documenting the changes. So the submarine that remains on the seabed may differ in significant details from the description below.

The Hull

The shape of the submarine's pressure hull is a simple cylinder with a cone attached at each end. The overall shape of the hull remained the same throughout the design and development process but the dimensions and details changed as the project progressed. The earliest sketch of the design shows a 30 ft (9.1 m) long boat with the cones and body of three equal lengths. Later designs extended the length to 40 ft (12.2 m) with 10 ft (3.0 m) cones then finally to a 40 ft (12.2 m) length and 12 ft (3.7 m) cones. The diameter of the central cylinder was initially 7 ft (2.1 m) but was later reduced to 6 ft 6 in (2.0 m). The central cylinder is made from sheets of rolled wrought iron, initially intended to be 1 inch (25.4 mm) in thickness but this was reduced to 3/4 inch (19 mm). Garrett did mention using steel plates for the hull in his 1878 patent as they would be stronger. Steel was commonly available at that date since the advent of the Bessemer process in 1855, but iron was used instead, perhaps because Cochran's were more used to working with it. The 16 ft (4.9 m) long main cylinder is formed from three rolled sheets of wrought iron riveted together along their long edges with each sheet forming 120° or one third of the cylinder. The longitudinal seams were single 6 in (152 mm) lap joints where the plates to be joined overlap each other while the transverse seams were made as double butt joints where the plates butt up against each other and are riveted together with a strap. Two or three shaped pieces of wrought iron form each cone, reducing to one single piece towards the point, noted as being made of 3/4 inch (19 mm) plate reducing to 5/8 in (15.9 mm) at the ends.

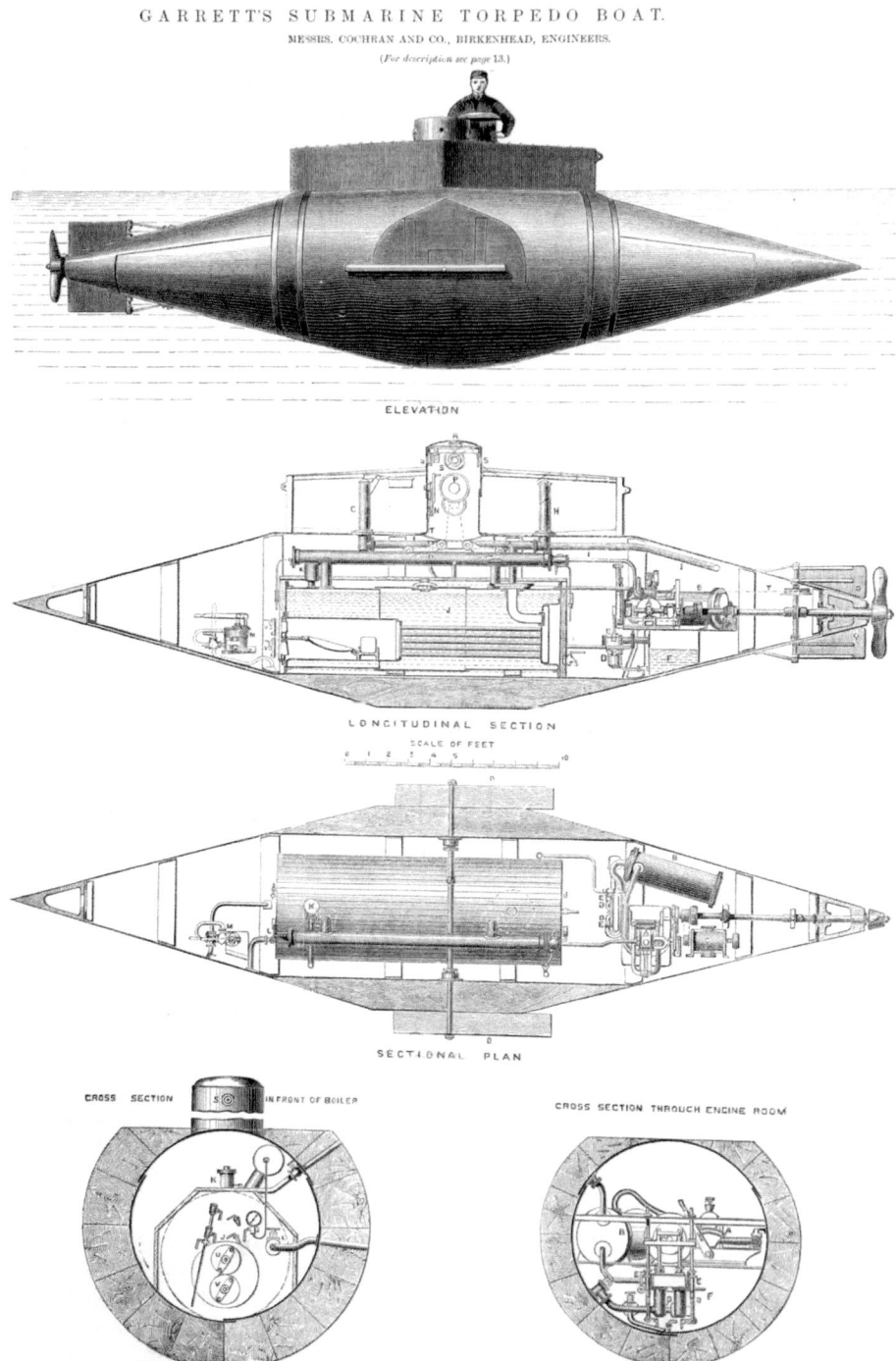

Figure 8: The plan of the Resurgam published in the journal The Engineer

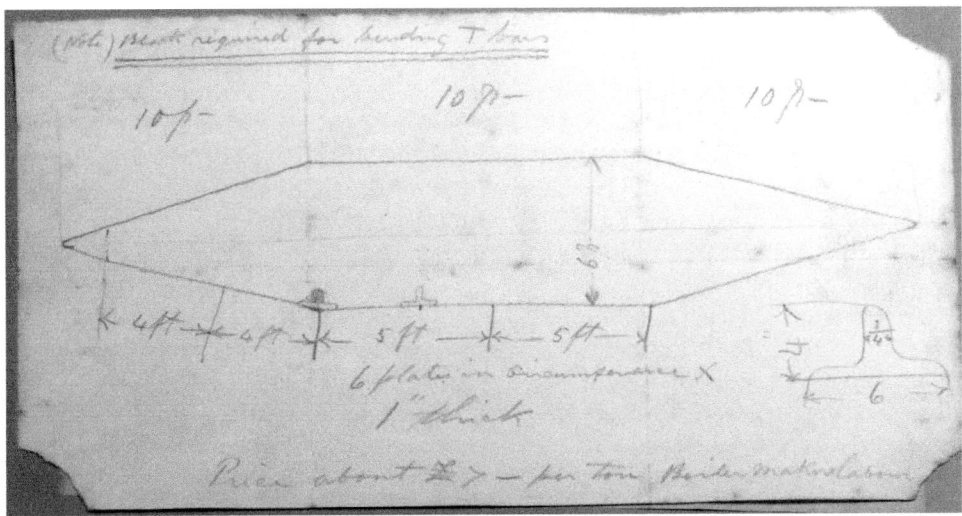

Figure 9: An early sketch of the Resurgam only 30 ft long and reinforced with T section iron frames (RNSM)

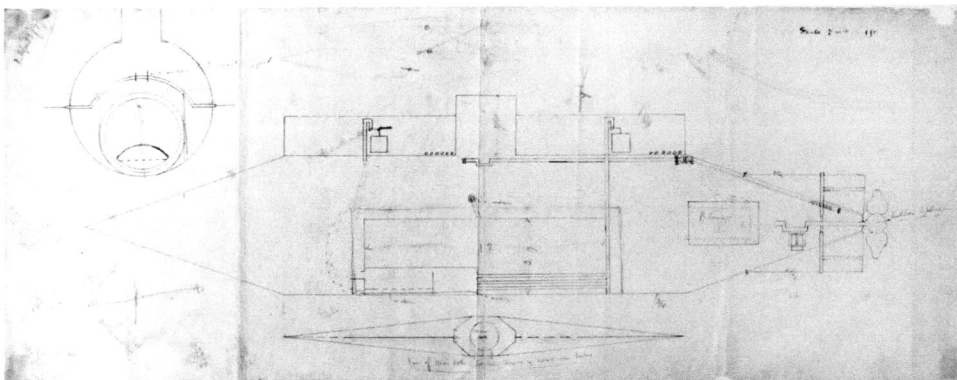

Figure 10: A modified sketch of the submarine by Jack Aitkin showing the boiler arrangement, snorkel, engine and blower (RNSM)

The specification says the nose cone was formed from a casting, this is a sensible design decision as forming the tip of the cone from plate iron would have been difficult. A small hole in the upper side of the nose cone is shown in the photograph, the purpose is unknown, but it may be matched with a similar hole on the underside to allow the nose cone to be free flooding. The drawing also shows a cast tail cone in the stern which would accommodate the stuffing box that provided the watertight seal for the propeller shaft.

The initial sketch shows two frames fitted in the central cylinder that were 'T' section iron rolled into a hoop 6 in (152 mm) wide with a 4 in (102 mm) high flange (Figure 9). The layout is not symmetrical so it is likely that two other frames would have been fitted into the cylinder at the opposite end, but the later quote from Cochran states that no internal frames were added to the pressure hull so we do not know what option was finally chosen. Internal frames would help withstand external hydrostatic pressure at depth but may have been omitted if the iron hull plating was considered strong enough on its own; frames would add unnecessary and unwelcome weight to an already heavy hull. The drawing in the journal *The Engineer* shows eight 10 in (254 mm) transverse bands in the form of hoops around the inside of the hull but these correspond to the joints in the hull plating so will be the butt joint plates mentioned earlier. The riveted cylinder plus cones structure was tested to 100 psi (6.9 bar), but it is likely that this was a hydrostatic test with pressure applied from the inside as this is how Cochran's would test their boilers. For this test the pressure hull would be completely filled with water, sealed up, and then the water pressure inside would be increased by pumping in more water through a fitting on the hull. Presuming the hull did not immediately burst under pressure the boilermakers would look for leaks in the joints between the plates then mark any that needed attention so repairs could be done when the hull had been depressurised and drained of water. Two deadlights (small round windows) were fitted in to the pressure hull on the centre line of the bow cone, one just forward of the main section and the other by the nose. A third deadlight fitted at the start of the taper on the stern end was noted by divers during recording of the hull of the submarine. It is not known if the portholes and deadlights had been fitted at the time the test was done; it seems unlikely as they would be designed to withstand pressure from the outside rather than the inside. It is not clear how much we can conclude about the safe working depth of the submarine based on a test where pressure was applied from the inside. However, if the same test pressure were applied as an external force the hull could cope with a differential pressure of 5.9 bar or 59 metres.

Figure 11: The replica Resurgam at Woodside showing the faired shape of the cladding timbers. The original timbers were baulks 18 in thick rather than the smaller planks used on the replica built by AMARC trainees in 1997

The *Resurgam's* pressure hull appears to have been built around the boiler used for propulsion leaving no room inside the cylindrical hull for anything else. It is curious that Garrett chose not to fit ballast tanks to the hull despite them being an essential feature of the prototype that survived through all of its design evolutions. This is the single most significant design decision that Garrett made as it affected the entire operation of the submarine and placed stringent requirements on the boats hydrodynamic capability and the output of the propulsion system.

Wood Cladding

The cylindrical part of the hull section was clad in fourteen 18 inch (0.46 m) thick oak timbers. The timbers would add volume to the hull and so increase the vessel's buoyancy, acting as the Victorian equivalent of the syntactic foam used on modern underwater vehicles. The individual timbers that formed the cladding were 16 ft (4.9 m) long and bevelled over a 4.5 ft (1.4 m) length at each end at the same 15.5° angle as the conical ends of the boat. The timbers were a truncated wedge or 'keystone' shape in section, with four timbers together forming a 90° angle round the cylinder. The photograph (Figure 11) shows the shaped timbers extending above each hydroplane to provide a flat surface for the hydroplane to sit against when the planes were angled for diving, the existing timbers being topped with an additional pyramid shaped timber piece. The upper part of the timbers was faired off level with the top of the pressure hull so the cladding timbers formed a flat deck. The timber cladding was held on to the hull using four iron straps, two 80 mm wide at the thin ends of the timbers and two more that were 160 mm wide fitted either side of the conning tower.

The two end straps are visible in the photograph while the inner two straps are laid into channels in the timbers and faired over with wood filling pieces. There is no evidence of any secondary means of fixing the timbers together but the timber cladding was bored through for pipes to take in water for the condenser and discharge to the sea. The timber cladding was not mentioned in Garrett's first designs or in the quote from the builder but it does appear in the original engineering drawings. Some aspect of the design changed during the design process which meant that the timber had to be added; this is discussed further in the chapter on Weight, Buoyancy and Dynamics.

Conning Tower and Fairing / Cutwater

In the top centre of the cylindrical section of the pressure hull is a conning tower 3 ft (0.9 m) tall and 2 ft (0.6 m) in diameter made of wrought iron. The drawing suggests that the tower was constructed from two cylindrical sections, with the lower section 2.4 ft (0.7 m) in diameter. The photographs of the submarine before launching provide no clues about how the tower was made as the possible join between the sections is hidden under the fairing. A join between two cylindrical sections was not recorded during the 1997 diver survey so it is likely that the conning tower was actually made in one piece. A sketch from the 1997 diver survey shows two U shaped straps bolted to the base of the conning tower which may be associated with the method of its attachment to the hull.

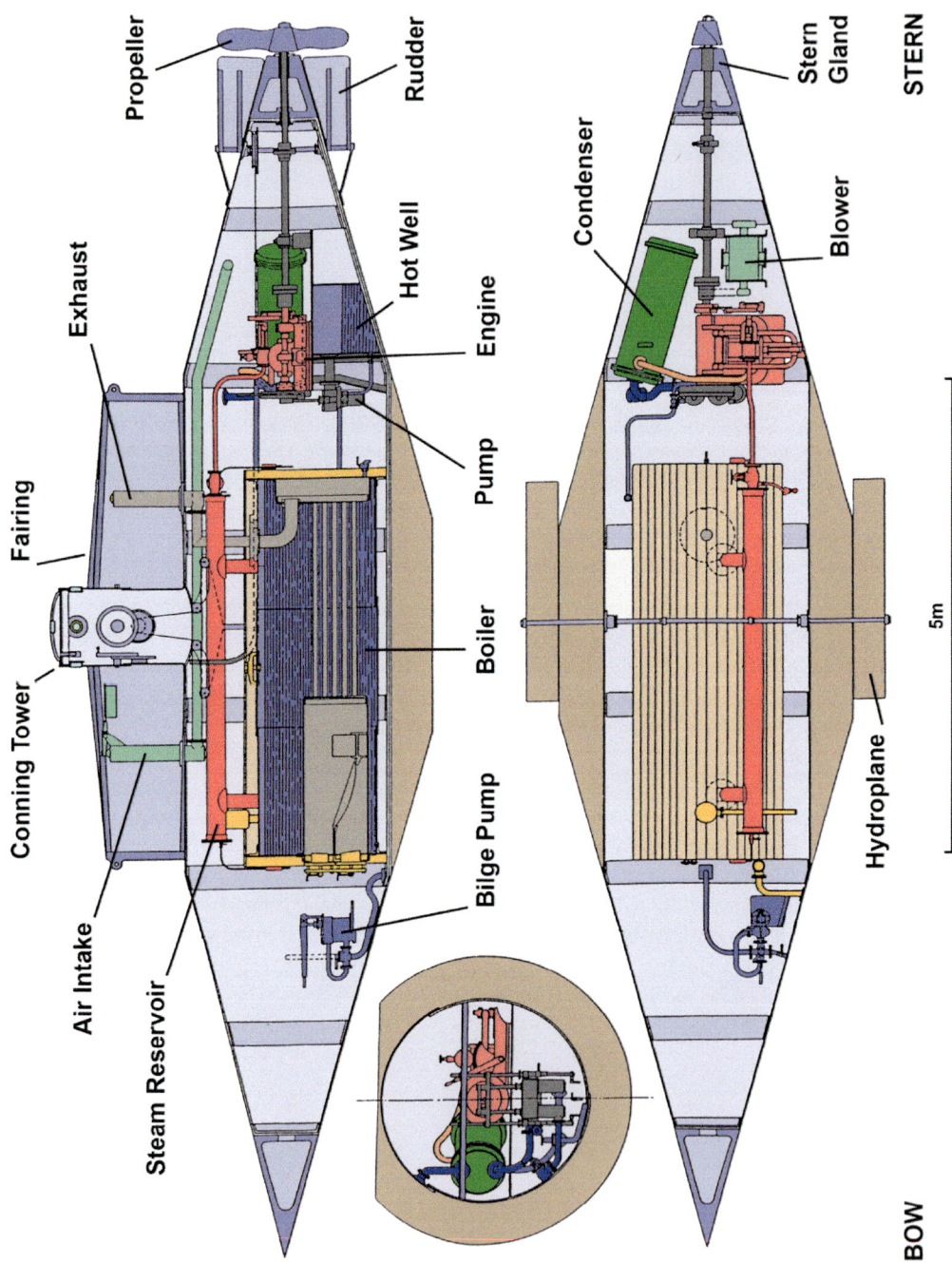

Figure 12: Plan, Elevation and Section of Resurgam

Figure 13: Detail from a photograph of the submarine showing the conning tower hatch

On the top of the tower was a 16 in diameter hatch or 'manhole' as Garrett described it. The hatch was either made of brass with a deadlight in the top and inscribed '*Garrett Submarine Boat, Resurgam, 1879. Cochran & Co., builders, Birkenhead*' or made of iron with a brass plate attached.

As can be seen in Figure 13, the hatch was mounted so that it opened horizontally towards the bow, swivelling on a pivot at the front of the conning tower, but the details of the hinge are unknown as is the means of securing the hatch at sea. Garrett's 1878 Patent for the prototype *Egg* submarine includes the statement that:

> '*I arrange the roof of the conning tower so that it is easily taken off if anything happens to the boat, so that the occupants can rise to the surface, being aided by life belts if desired.*'

Being a significant safety feature it is possible that this idea was carried over to the hatch fitted to the top of the conning tower on *Resurgam*. Garrett specified that the hatch could be fastened from the inside only but the design notes from 10th April state that it would be fitted with '*1 manhole screw inside and out*' (Figure 14) suggesting that the hatch could be closed from the outside. This small and seemingly insignificant design feature noted by Wareing is crucial to the story of the loss of this submarine.

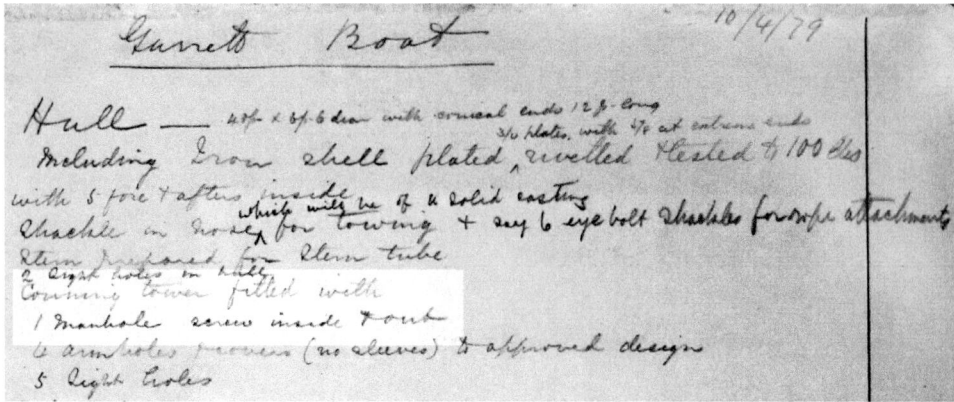

Figure 14: Specification for construction noting the conning tower '1 Manhole screw inside and out' (RNSM)

The design also called for a 'lookout' or porthole to be fitted in each of the four cardinal points around the conning tower, a deadlight in the top hatch and one pair of sleeves on each side.

Sleeves were fitted to Garrett's prototype submarine but the decision to add them to *Resurgam* was later dropped. The vessel was piloted from within the conning tower; the helmsman stood on the wood cladding over the boiler in the 1.9 m high space inside the tower and attempted to see where he was going through the tiny porthole in front. Vessel heading was controlled using a small steering wheel attached to the front of the tower and depth was controlled by setting the hydroplane angles using a similar hand wheel mounted on the side. Given the small size of the portholes, the position at which the operator stood and the constant heat and humidity when closed down, steering the vessel in heavy seas would have proved extremely difficult.

A fairing or cutwater formed from riveted sheet iron was constructed around the conning tower. The fairing was open to the sea so would fill with water as the submarine dived and drain out again when the submarine surfaced. The double wedge shaped fairing was 15 ft (4.6 m) long overall, 2.7 ft (0.8 m) tall at the ends and 3.1 ft (0.9 m) high in the middle where it was attached to the conning tower. The fairing was built from iron plate riveted to an internal iron framework that was securely attached to the hull; the frame must have been strongly built as the tow point for the submarine was fitted high up on the leading edge of the fairing. It is thought that the top of the fairing was covered with a flat, triangular plate but none of the drawings or photographs can confirm this. Under the fairing were the air intake and the exhaust for the engine so some means of access would have been necessary for maintenance work on the intake and vent valves. The four straps holding the wood cladding to the hull passed under four matching recesses on the bottom edge of the fairing, the recesses were fitted to allow the fairing to flood at the start of a dive and for it to drain out once back on the surface. There must also have been holes in the triangular top plates on the fairing to allow air to get to the engine air intake at the forward end and to allow exhaust gases to escape from the aft fairing. The wedge-shaped fairing would partially streamline the conning tower and so reduce drag underwater but its main role was to act as a cutwater when the boat was running on the surface. The fairing would keep waves from washing against the front of the conning tower; this would reduce the amount of water entering the submarine if the conning tower hatch was open and it would allow the helmsman to see more easily through the tiny forward facing porthole. The fairing was free flooding and was not part of the pressure hull so did not provide any additional buoyancy. It would take time to drain the water out of the space inside the fairing after the boat surfaced which would delay the submarine's arrival on the surface.

The Rudders and Hydroplanes

Two triangular unbalanced vertical rudders 3.1 ft (0.9 m) by 1.4 ft (0.4 m) were fitted on the stern to enable the boat to turn to port or starboard. The rudders were connected to a single shaft passing vertically through the pressure hull through two stuffing boxes while the two ends of the spindle were supported by brackets attached to the outside of the hull. On the inside of the submarine the rudder shaft was fitted with a wheel that was actuated by wire or chain connected to a small steering wheel in the conning tower.

A pair of balanced wooden hydroplanes 7.3 ft (2.2 m) long and 1 ft (0.3 m) wide were fitted on each side of the hull and were intended to '*raise or lower the level at which the boat would float*'. Confusingly these hydroplanes were also referred to as 'rudders' by Garrett. The hydroplanes were fitted amidships on the centreline of the hull, connected to a single iron shaft running athwartships through stuffing boxes into the hull and connected via a chain to a hand wheel in the conning tower. The shaft joining the hydroplanes was curved in the middle so that it could pass over the top of the boiler, but as the hydroplanes were angled downwards the curved portion of the spindle moved forwards and would eventually come in contact with the boiler top, which would limit the range of travel of the hydroplanes. It has been suggested that Garrett deserves credit for the invention of the hydroplane but he was beaten to this by a number of early submarines including the CSS H.L. *Hunley*.

The Lamm 'Fireless' Steam Engine

One of the more unusual aspects of Garrett's submarine was the use of the 'fireless' steam engine. The working version of his prototype submarine was powered using foot operated treadles but Garrett would have known from other previous submarine designs that human power was not enough. There were few mechanical propulsion systems available to Garrett at this time and none were reliable enough for use in a submarine other than the steam engine which in 1879 was well-known technology. The fireless version of the steam engine chosen to be fitted inside the submarine was a novel variant that used a different boiler arrangement, so when we refer to the 'fireless engine' this includes the boiler and pipe work as well as the engine itself. The novel component in the propulsion system was a steam reservoir so the name 'fireless engine' is in some ways misleading as the engine itself was a standard design. The explorer Sydney Wignall who searched for the *Resurgam* in 1978 called the fireless engine fitted in the boat a *'breakthrough in submarine propulsion'* and archaeologist Michael Bowyer referred to it as a *'true prize'* since the discovery of *Resurgam* may represent the only known surviving example of a fireless steam engine.

In a conventional Victorian marine steam engine, fuel is burned in the furnace of a boiler to heat water to produce steam and the steam is piped to a reciprocating engine which is then used to drive a propeller. The fireless system differs from this simply by adding an accumulator or steam reservoir between the boiler and the steam engine; the accumulator is used to store superheated water that can be turned to steam when needed and used to drive the engine. The boiling point of water rises with increasing pressure so the reservoir can be used to contain superheated water so long as the pressure is maintained. Opening a valve in the pipe that connects the accumulator to the engine lowers the pressure inside the accumulator which causes useful steam to be generated. The loss of steam through the engine reduces the pressure inside the accumulator causing more steam to be created; this process carries on until the superheated water is used up or until the temperature drops below a useful level.

Eugene Lamm patented the fireless engine on the 30th July 1872, as an *'improvement to supplying steam in travelling engines'* and in his own words described the invention:

> *"The object of my invention is to heat above the atmospheric pressure water contained in a close vessel or reservoir... the steam having been previously generated under pressure in a stationary boiler. By this process I avoid discharging the water on the car, the temperature of which was lowered by the steam expended in working the engine during the trip. Thus instead of replacing the same water in the reservoir by other and hotter water taken from the stationary boiler, I cause steam of the required temperature to rush into and condense until the pristine force or heat of the water is restored"*

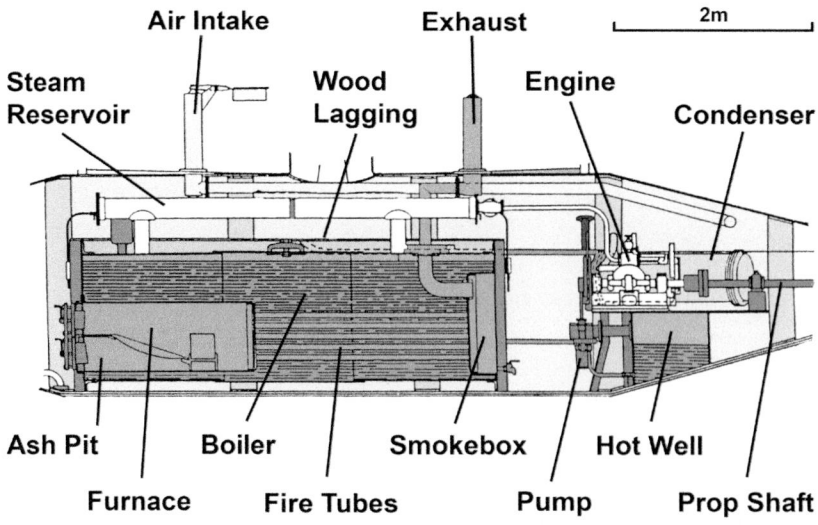

Figure 15: Diagram of the propulsion system

A fireless engine was used on the New Orleans and Carrollton Railway. The accumulator on the engine was filled with water which was then superheated by passing steam through it from a stationary boiler alongside the track. Once the water was at the right temperature the boiler was disconnected and the reservoir of steam was used to provide motive power. This system had advantages in urban areas because the fireless engine did not produce sparks or hot cinders that could start fires, it was quieter than a traditional steam locomotive and it did not produce unpleasant smells and soot. The drawback was that the fireless railway engine could only be refuelled using dedicated wayside boilers so it could run out of steam if it was not managed correctly.

The coal-fired boiler Garrett fitted inside the submarine's hull was 45 inches (1.14 m) in diameter and 12 ft (3.65 m) in length and held three tons of water, with a safety pressure of 150 psi (10.2 bar) (Figure 15). Once the water was heated to the correct temperature it was transferred to a steam reservoir where it could be stored as latent energy; when necessary the throttle valve for the engine could be opened allowing 15% of the stored water to turn into steam at 30-40 psi (2.0 to 2.8 bar) which was piped to the steam engine and used to drive the propeller. The specification from Garrett included:

> 'In addition to the above there remains a reservoir for compressed gas which must stand a pressure of 1000 lb. and which can be got from Birmingham in the shape of steel tubes which could conveniently be stowed in the boat.'

The furnace that heated the water in the boiler would have to be cleverly constructed so that pressure could be maintained inside while more fuel was added. The furnace was 2 ft (0.6 m) in diameter by 5 ft (1.5 m) in length and had an air tight front hatch; it is noted in the correspondence that this was to be constructed of steel. There were five fire tubes 1.5 inches (38.1 mm) in diameter and 6 ft (1.8 m) long which connected to a smokebox, the smoke from the furnace vented through the smokebox to an exhaust pipe beneath the aft fairing. The boiler took up most of the room inside the cylindrical part of the hull; it was lagged in wood so it was possible to climb over it once it was at working temperature but even so the temperature inside the submarine must have been excessive. The plans suggest that the steam reservoir was not lagged so this would have acted as a large heat radiator inside the boat; this would have been evident in sea trials so this may be lagged in the real submarine. Even loading the coal fuel would have been difficult as the sole entry point to the vessel was through the conning tower and the only way to load the coal would be to pass it down through the tower, through the small gap over the boiler and into the coal bunker in the bow.

The Engine

Garrett had limited requirements for the engine, simply requesting that it should generate 6 horsepower (4.5kW) from a pressure of 30 to 40 psi (2.0 to 2.8 bar) using a single piston and be situated as close to the propeller as possible. The company noted that the engine needed to have a great economy in the use of steam so it was to be fitted with link motion based on Stephenson valve gear. Steam energy would be saved as the eccentric turn of the Stephenson gear would be powered partially by its own motion.

The engine fitted inside the submarine was made of cast iron and had a cylinder with an 8 in (203 mm) diameter and 8 in stroke; the large piston diameter was required because of the low steam pressure available. The type of steam engine that is most familiar is the direct acting type where the power from the piston is applied directly to the crankshaft via a connecting rod. The engine in *Resurgam* was unusual as it was of the return connecting rod or back acting type where the connecting rods are led backwards from the crosshead to the crankshaft; this design saved a considerable amount of space because the steam engine was effectively folded in half. In *Resurgam* the engine was arranged with the cylinder lying horizontally and the piston emerged from the cylinder towards the port side where it joined two connecting rods at the crosshead. The connecting rod was 'U' shaped with two long arms that ran either side of the cylinder, one attached to the crankshaft and the other connected to the pumps. The return connecting rod type engine was used in early steamships where space was limited because it allowed the cylinders to be brought closer to the crank shaft.[1]

> **The Invention of the Snorkel**
>
> Many authors credit the Dutch with the invention of the submarine snorkel as they had been experimenting with them as early as 1938. The Germans became aware of the design after they invaded Holland in 1940 and captured Dutch submarines fitted with the device. However, a snorkel was not fitted on a U-boat until 1943 when the first boat fitted was *U-58*. But the Dutch were not the first. James Richardson patented a design for a snorkel during WW1 (Richardson 1917) when he was an Assistant Manager at Scotts Shipbuilding and Engineering Company in Scotland. Although the patent was granted the Royal Navy chose not to use it. Garrett's design for the snorkel predates the patent by 38 years, but earlier still the USS *Alligator* built in 1862 had air tubes and a pump to ventilate the boat while still underwater. However this submarine was propelled by 18 men rather than an engine, so Garrett may still be the first to use a snorkel to ventilate an engine in a powered submarine.

The connecting rod was made of wrought iron while the bearings would be of gunmetal, an alloy of copper, tin and zinc. Gunmetal was useful in marine fittings as it was resistant to corrosion from steam and salt water so it was ideal for use in a submarine.

Condenser

The condenser is a heat exchanger for condensing exhaust steam from the engine back into liquid water that can be pumped back into the boiler to be reused. The first marine steam engines used a jet of cold sea water to condense the steam which resulted in a mix of fresh and sea water being fed back to the boiler. The mix of salt and fresh water caused internal corrosion so a better solution was required. The surface condenser was a later improvement; here cold sea water is pumped around a series of tubes inside the condenser which is also supplied with hot exhaust steam from the engine.

---

[1] The Engineer 1882, Sennett & Oram 1908

The steam rapidly condenses on the cold tubes before the resulting fresh water is collected in the hot well before being sent back to the boiler. The fresh boiler water is always kept separate from the cooling sea water which reduces the formation of scale within the engine and boiler and minimises salt water corrosion. Garrett was specific about the condenser as he wanted it to sit between the engine and the boiler, but close enough to the boiler without interfering with its efficiency (Figure 16). The condenser and boiler were to be considered as one, as such *'their centre of gravity should coincide with the centre of the boat'*.[2] Aitken's notes on the subject are brief as he mentions only that the condenser be of *'ample dimension'* and conveniently located.[3] The condenser was located on the starboard side of the vessel connected to two reciprocating pumps, one to push cooling sea water through the condenser and the other to pump water back to the boiler from the hot well, with the sump tank being used to collect condensate.

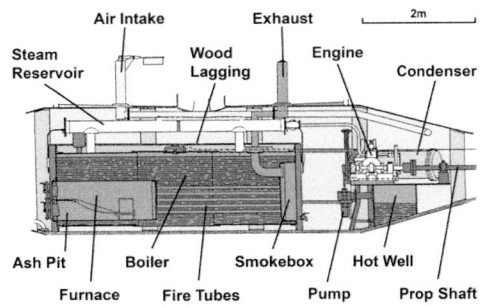

Figure 16: Diagram of the propulsion system

The Blower

The large volume of water inside the boiler would take a very long time to heat up, but forcing air over the furnace would raise the temperature inside and allow steam to be raised more quickly. Garrett specified that a Roots-type blower or air pump be fitted as near to the engine as possible, to be belt-driven from the engine but with the ability to be operated by hand when required. When firing the engine from cold the blower was initially operated by hand but was switched to engine power once the steam pressure in the boiler reached 30-40 psi (2.0-2.7 bar). This suggests that there was a clutch between the engine and the propeller so that the engine could be run to drive the blower without the propeller going round.

When the submarine was running on the surface with the conning tower hatch closed, air was drawn in to the submarine through an intake fitted under the fairing on the foredeck, a feature that later became known as a snorkel or snort. The snorkel was connected directly to the inside of the submarine so any water passing down the snorkel tube would end up inside the boat and if too much water was taken on board the submarine could sink. To counteract this problem there was a brass float valve on the top of the snorkel which would close automatically when a wave passed over the top; it is also likely that this valve could be closed manually when diving or in an emergency so the lives of the submariners were not reliant on a simple float valve. The snorkel in *Resurgam* appears be the first recorded use of this device to ventilate a submarine engine.

---

[2] Garrett 1879
[3] Garrett 1879

The design of the ventilation system would also need to maximise the circulation of what little air there was inside the boat. We do know that any air entering the hull would have to pass through the furnace, into the smokebox then escape out of the hull through the exhaust pipe. The drawing in the journal *The Engineer* (Figure 15) shows the snorkel connected by a pipe to the Roots blower and the output of the blower vented inside the boat. Air would then flow inside the hull from the stern to the bows, scavenging its own engine fumes, and then make its way out through the furnace. However, the intake would only work if the blower was running. Any water that entered the snorkel would make its way straight into the pump unless the pipe included a water trap.

Price reported that during trials the crew complained of pressure on their ear drums; this increase in pressure may have been caused by the blower if it were venting straight into the main hull. Under normal conditions the pressure inside the hull would only be slightly above ambient with the blower running as the pumped air could escape through the furnace and out through the exhaust pipe. If the exhaust pipe was fitted with an automatic valve like the intake and the valve closed as a wave passed over, then the pressure in the hull would rise momentarily, before dropping quickly when the exhaust opened again. Adding to the heat and the fumes, pain from rapid air compression and decompression would have made working inside the submarine extremely unpleasant.

Propeller

A 3 ft 6 in (1.0 m) diameter cast iron propeller was mounted on the outside of the hull and was directly connected to the engine via a solid iron propeller shaft with no intermediate gearing other than a clutch. The bearings for the propeller shaft were housed in a stuffing box situated in a casting that formed the apex of the cone at the rear of the boat. The stuffing box is a housing that contains a gland seal around the propeller shaft that stops water from entering the hull yet still allows the propeller to turn.

It is often thought that *Resurgam* left for trials with a two bladed propeller but in the picture of *Resurgam* at Birkenhead two blades of a three-bladed propeller can be seen with the boat's stern hiding the third blade (Figure 17). The confusion may arise as the drawing in the journal *The Engineer* clearly shows a two bladed propeller with a very coarse pitch, but the illustration above the section drawing shows a three bladed propeller. A sketch from the 1997 survey shows that *Resurgam* sank fitted with a three-bladed propeller but as the blades were broken off the size and pitch are unknown.

Figure 17: Detail of a photograph of Resurgam showing the three-bladed propeller. The hull obscures the third blade.

By 1879 much was already known about the use of screw propellers. The first steamship fitted with a screw propeller was the *Archimedes* in 1839; she was built as a technology demonstrator to highlight the superiority of the screw propeller over earlier and less efficient paddlewheel technology. The famous tug-of-war between the paddle ship *Alecto* and the screw sloop HMS *Rattler* that publicly demonstrated the propeller's supremacy had happened 34 years before *Resurgam* was built.[4] In that time many experiments had been done on the propeller and the results published so Garrett would have known something about the principles of operation.

Garrett would need to balance a number of factors when designing the propeller for *Resurgam*. The propeller must be designed for the particular engine fitted inside the boat to ensure that the combination of engine and propeller provided the optimum thrust at the designed operating speed. The propeller would need to be of the correct diameter - if it was too small it may not provide enough thrust and if too big the propeller becomes unwieldy to mount on the stern of the submarine. The number and pitch of the propeller blades is also important. Having just two blades on the submarine's propeller would be a disadvantage as the total blade area would be small but increasing to three or four blades on the same diameter propeller provides more working area and thus more thrust. If the pitch or angle of the blades is coarse then the propeller will be trying to move a lot of water with each revolution: a fine pitch would move less water but also provide less thrust. A two bladed propeller would also cause the stern of the boat to vibrate. The two vertical rudders mounted on the stern would disturb the flow of water behind them as the submarine moves forward, the two propeller blades would enter and leave this disturbed flow at the same time so induced vibration would occur at every half turn of the propeller. With a three bladed propeller only one blade would be in a patch of disturbed water at any time so the induced vibration would be reduced. Garrett had commented after the first sea trials that; *'we are going to make a series of experiments with various propellers'* [5]; and in doing so he would have to balance the engine's capability with the propeller diameter, number of blades and blade pitch to produce an optimum design.

---

[4] Gardiner 1992
[5] Garrett 1879

The *Resurgam* Submarine in Use

Weight and Buoyancy

For a submarine to work effectively the weight of the boat and its buoyancy must be in harmony; if the submarine is too heavy it will simply sink to the bottom and if it is too buoyant then it will not submerge at all. If the weight of the submarine is equal to the buoyancy then the submarine can dive beneath the waves and drive itself back to the surface, an ideal situation known as being neutrally buoyant which is remarkably hard to achieve in practice. Most submarines are fitted with large ballast tanks which are used to greatly increase buoyancy while the submarine is on the surface, but can be flooded at will to allow the boat to submerge. By filling the ballast tanks with water the buoyancy is decreased which allows the submarine to sink while pumping or blowing compressed air into the tanks forces the water out, increasing buoyancy and making the submarine float. When the main ballast tanks are empty of water the submarine is in 'surface trim' and with the tanks full of water the submarine is in 'diving trim'. Surface trim is used when the submarine is motoring on the surface or when tied up alongside a dock as there is plenty of extra buoyancy to keep the submarine afloat. Diving trim is only adopted just before the submarine is to submerge. Garrett's first submarine was fitted with ballast tanks that could be filled by opening a valve inside the boat and emptied using a hand pump but *Resurgam* was not fitted with any ballast tanks at all.

Even with the ballast tanks full of water, many submarines retain a small positive or 'reserve' buoyancy so they naturally float with just a little of the hull visible above the surface. To submerge, the boats are driven underwater using a combination of hydroplanes and forward propulsion. A submarine with reserve buoyancy needs to keep moving forward to stay under water; if the main motor stops then the boat will slowly float back to the surface which is a useful safety feature in the event of a motor failure. In diving trim the submarine only need take on a small amount of extra weight for it to submerge, just enough to overcome the reserve buoyancy, so if a leak occurs or water enters the submarine through an open hatch it may only take a small amount of water to sink it. Crucially, ballast tanks were not included in the design for *Resurgam* so her surface trim was the same as her diving trim. *Resurgam* was designed with enough reserve buoyancy to support the weight of the conning tower and fairing allowing the upperworks to remain visible on the surface when the submarine was stationary. This turns out to be a considerable amount of buoyancy that had to be overcome for the vehicle to be able to dive and remain underwater.

For *Resurgam*, weight and buoyancy calculations would have been completed by her designers and some of the original design documents in the Royal Navy Submarine Museum include these figures. Because a hull of any given volume can only support a certain amount of weight, the size of the boat was dependant on what machinery and stores needed to be carried. In effect, Garrett would have to work out how much the boiler and engine weighed and then design a hull to fit round it that would support that weight. A bigger hull would be more expensive to manufacture and would be more difficult to handle at sea so the hull needed to be as small as possible while still being able to fit the machinery inside and support the design weight when afloat. None of the initial design documents include the timber cladding that was fitted around the hull but it is shown in Cochran's later engineering drawing that was used to build the boat. This was a drastic step; adding the timber around the hull would make the submarine wider and heavier which would reduce the top speed on the surface and underwater. Some crucial aspect of the design changed between first concept and the final version that required the timber to be added. The reason for adding the timber given in a newspaper article was simply '*for the purpose of protection*' [6], but this makes little sense as only the centre section of the hull is covered in timber leaving the bow and stern cones exposed. It is more likely that the final design of the submarine was too heavy and the timber was added to increase the volume of the hull which in turn would increase the buoyancy. To investigate this idea we can recalculate the weight and buoyancy based on the as-built dimensions of *Resurgam*. The main pressure hull was constructed from 3/4 inch wrought iron plate. By calculating the area of the plate from the known dimensions we can estimate the mass of iron to be 8922kg or 8.8 Imperial tons, which is close to the 9 tons estimated by Cochran & Co. on 10th April 1879.

Item	**Mass**
Pressure hull, calculated	8922 kg
Boiler, 3 tons estimated	3048 kg
Machinery, 1.5 tons estimated	1524 kg
Sundries, 1 ton estimated	1016 kg
Water, 3 tons estimated	3048 kg
Coal, 2.5 tons estimated	2540 kg
Ballast, 1 ton estimated	1016 kg
Crew, estimated	255 kg
Fairing, calculated	260 kg
TOTAL mass	21630 kg
Volume of the hull	*22554 litres*
TOTAL Buoyancy (seawater)	23005 kg
Reserve (buoyancy - mass)	1375 kg

---

[6] Manchester Courier 1879b

With the submarine on the surface the calculated reserve buoyancy is 1375kg. When the submarine is underwater the buoyancy of the conning tower must be added to the buoyancy of the hull. The tower weighs approximately 260kg but has a buoyancy of 270kg which suggests that it was deliberately designed to be neutrally buoyant. This would be an advantage when diving as the buoyancy of the boat would not change dramatically in the transition from being afloat to being submerged. This leaves the reserve buoyancy to support only the fairing when the submarine was on the surface: a weight of just 260 kg. Sueter quotes a figure of 100lbs (45.4kg) for the reserve buoyancy[7] but unfortunately does not quote the source. This is 17% of the estimated required buoyancy which would only support a similar fraction of the fairing and conning tower above the water.

The original design calculations showed that the buoyancy of the submarine would support its own weight with the upperworks out of the water, but this left no room for errors. If the propulsion system was heavier than expected the additional weight would leave *Resurgam* too heavy for the size of her hull. Excess weight has been a perennial problem for all small submarine designs; the designer of the Royal Navy A class submarine spent three days in the drawing office removing metal from stanchions and upperworks on the hull just to lose half a ton from a 200 ton submarine.[8] If nothing could be removed from the boat to lighten it then the only solution would be to increase buoyancy by making the hull bigger so that it displaced more water. Making the iron hull bigger was an expensive solution but adding timber to the outside would be cheap and easy to achieve.

The addition of the timber increased the submarine's mass but it added more buoyancy giving Garrett 3.1 tonnes of additional buoyancy that he could use. This extra buoyancy may have been used to compensate for heavier machinery but it may also have been needed to make the submarine more stable.

Item	Mass
Timber volume, calculated	*11.5 m³*
Timber density	*740 kg/m³*
Timber mass	8515 kg
TOTAL mass (submarine + timber)	30145 kg
Volume of the hull + timber	*33117 litres*
TOTAL Buoyancy	33780 kg
Reserve (buoyancy - mass)	3635 kg
Additional buoyancy (Reserve-520kg)	3115 kg

---
[7] Sueter M. 1907, p50
[8] Bacon 1940, p71

Stability

As well as considering the weight and buoyancy of the submarine we must also consider where the centre of gravity and centre of buoyancy are located on the hull. If one end of the submarine is heavier than the other it will tend to pitch downwards in that direction so it is essential to keep the submarine evenly balanced. The boat also needs to be heavier at the bottom than at the top of the hull otherwise it will roll heavily at sea or simply turn upside down.

The *Resurgam* submarine was symmetrical in shape fore and aft, short in length and circular in section, so it would tend to roll and pitch very easily when on the surface, bobbing about like a buoy. This is a well known problem; it is difficult to provide modern submarines with sufficient heel or roll stability because of their shape so they suffer from slow heavy rolling when on the surface. To keep the boat upright the centre of gravity has to be lower than the centre of buoyancy. For cylindrical-hulled submarines the centre of buoyancy is usually along the axis of the cylinder so heavy items like the boiler and ballast have to be placed below the axis, keeping them low down in the hull. The heaviest object in the *Resurgam* was the six ton boiler and this was placed in the middle of the vessel along the centreline. The boiler was mounted as low as possible but a quarter of its mass still remained above the centre of buoyancy in the vertical axis. The heavy steam condenser and the heavy steam engine were placed aft of the boiler on the centreline of the hull. The engine was mounted horizontally and had to be attached directly to the propeller shaft, which unfortunately put this considerable mass of iron high up in the hull close to the vertical centre of buoyancy. The condenser was placed at the same level on the starboard side of the hull so it counterbalanced the weight of the engine on the port side, but this also added more weight high up.

Other factors come in to play when considering the submarine in use. The 2.5 tons of coal used for fuel was stored inside the hull in the point of the forward cone. As far forward as possible and many metres from the centre of the hull, the weight of coal would have a considerable effect on the trim of the boat. As the coal was used up the submarine, and the bow in particular, would become progressively lighter, the boat would float higher out of the water and it would start to trim bow up. There would be no way of compensating for this loss of mass up forward other than moving iron ballast blocks further forward because the boat was not fitted with the trim tanks usually used for this purpose.

If that were not enough to concern Garrett, another factor he had to consider was the free surface effect of water in the boiler and bilge and how that would affect longitudinal stability. If the boiler was full of water then any change in the attitude of the boat would not affect the centre of gravity as when full there would be nowhere for the water to run. If the boiler was partly empty then the water would be able to flow to one end or the other which would shift its centre of gravity. If the boiler were half full and the bow tipped down a little, the water in the boiler would run forward, increasing the mass forward and making the bow tip down even further so even more water moved in the same direction. Any movement of the water in a partly filled boiler could exacerbate the pitch of the boat in a rough sea as the water sloshed about inside, constantly moving the centre of gravity fore and aft. The same problem would exist with any water that collected in the bilge but its destabilising effect would be magnified as it was not constrained by the ends of the boiler and was free to run the full length of the boat. For this reason I expect that the crewman up forward was kept busy ensuring that bilge water was kept to a minimum and the pump near the engine could be used to remove any bilge water that collected in the stern.

It is not known why Garrett chose to add timber cladding to the hull but one possible reason for adding extra buoyancy was to allow Garrett to add more ballast where it was needed. Iron ballast blocks added low down in the bilge at the forward end would counteract the weight of the condenser and engine in the stern so the little boat would sit upright and on an even keel when afloat on the surface. The initial design may have had too much weight high up in the hull causing the boat to be unstable, so more ballast weight would need to be added low down in the hull to lower the centre of gravity and help cure this problem. The stability would have been further increased if Garrett had added timber only to the top of the hull rather than underneath as well. As he decided not to do this it is likely that the reason for adding the timber was not for curing a stability problem. The timber cladding does not appear in the initial designs but does appear in the build plans which were drawn before the submarine was built and before any stability problems were uncovered. Thus it is likely that the timber was added to correct a buoyancy problem rather than any problems with stability.

The *Resurgam* sailed without any armament so perhaps Garrett was thinking ahead when he added the timber cladding. Perhaps Garrett thought he would need the additional buoyancy to support a pair of heavy torpedoes on the outside of the hull. However, it may have been the additional ballast he needed to keep the vessel upright; each Whitehead torpedo weighed 383kg and they would have to be mounted high up on the outside of the hull so they could be reloaded at sea. Carrying two heavy torpedoes high up on the hull without the extra ballast low down in the hull would make the submarine unstable. If just one torpedo was launched and the mass was taken off one side only then without enough ballast the submarine would simply roll on its side.

There is no record of how stable *Resurgam* was at sea. But we can get a clue from a quote from a contemporary account of one of Garrett's later submarines, the Turkish *Nordenfelt II* (*Abdul Hamid*), which says that this longer vessel suffered greatly from longitudinal instability:

> 'Nothing could be imagined more unstable than this Turkish boat. The moment she left the horizontal position the water in her boiler and her tanks surged forwards and backwards and increased the angle of inclination. She was perpetually working up and down like a scale beam, and no human vigilance could keep her on an even keel for half a minute at a time.'

Life Support and the Pneumatophore

Another problem for Garrett to solve was how to keep the three man crew alive for some hours in a closed submarine that contained just 18 cubic metres (m³) of breathable air. When the submarine was stationary the conning tower hatch could be left open which allowed at least some of the air inside the submarine to circulate. With the hatch shut at sea the inside of the submarine would be ventilated using the Roots blower but only in calm conditions as even small waves would cause the air intake to shut automatically. Underwater there would be no means of replenishing the air in the submarine once the snorkel was submerged.

Gas Calculations

At complete rest and in a non-stressed state, a 70 kg person will breathe at a rate of 7.5 litres per minute and exhale air at 17% oxygen (O_2) and 3.2% carbon dioxide (CO_2). This results in a 'resting' oxygen uptake of 0.3 litres of O_2 per minute and a resting CO_2 discharge of 0.24 litres per minute. However, the rate of breathing is primarily triggered by the carbon dioxide content of inspired air as higher carbon dioxide levels trigger faster respiration rates. A significant increase in activity levels will also cause an increase in these rates so a person walking uses 25 litres per minute with 1.2 litres of O_2 taken up and 0.96 litres of CO_2 discharged per minute.

Breathing rate becomes faster as the carbon dioxide content of the inspired air increases. Normal air is 0.03% carbon dioxide (CO_2) and effects are noticed on the body as this percentage increases. The exposure limit for this gas is 0.5%. Headaches and an increased rate of breathing occur at 1% CO_2 concentration and the short-term exposure limit is 3% which results in a doubling of the normal breathing rate. Panting and intoxication occur above 5% CO_2 with unconsciousness occurring at about 10%. Normal air is 21% oxygen (O_2) and adverse effects on the body are noticeable as the percentage of this gas in the breathing mix decreases. The normal lower working limit is 19% O_2 and at 18% there is a slight increase in breathing effort while at 16% a flame lamp will go out. At 14% a person suffers emotional upset, impaired judgement and faulty co-ordination. At 12% cardiac damage can occur along with vomiting and at 10% a person would lapse into unconsciousness then death.

However, the combined physiological cost to the body of simultaneous low oxygen and high carbon dioxide levels will be greater than that if only one or the other were to occur and the problem would be further exacerbated if the imperfect seals on the boiler furnace leak fumes into the hull. It can be shown that for a person breathing at a rate of 25 l/m within a confined space of one cubic metre, an O_2 level of 18% will be reached at 29 minutes. But the CO_2 levels will reach the exposure limit of 0.5% in just 6 minutes and the 'upper' working limit of 1.25% in 15 minutes.

This indicates that the air supply is governed by the rate of build-up of carbon dioxide and not the drop in oxygen. Based on these figures our three submariners sharing 18m³ would reach dangerous CO_2 levels in just 90 minutes.

For the crew to breathe they would need a supply of oxygen gas (O_2) and a means of removing the carbon dioxide gas (CO_2) that they exhaled. The submarine did not include a built-in life support system so without some other means for providing breathable air the length of time the submarine could stay submerged was dependent on how quickly the oxygen was used up or how quickly the carbon dioxide level increased. Knowing the volume of air in the submarine and estimating breathing rates we can calculate how long the crew could remain inside the submarine unaided.

The calculations suggest that the crew could remain closed up inside the submarine for just 90 minutes, see the note on Gas Calculations. The solution Garrett proposed to this problem was for each of the crew to have a personal life support system. Garrett studied chemistry as an undergraduate and later studied the chemistry of breathing, so he knew that caustic potash (potassium hydroxide, KOH) will absorb carbon dioxide so it could be used to remove this gas from air in a confined space. Unfortunately potassium hydroxide is highly corrosive, it can severely irritate and burn the skin and breathing it will irritate the lungs leading to a build up of fluid. Experimenting and using this chemical would have been risky but in 1877 Garrett developed a breathing system that used caustic potash to absorb CO_2 and included an undisclosed attachment for supplying oxygen. The exhaled air passed through a tube into a 'knapsack' which contained the chemicals where it was purified:

> *For the purpose of breathing, the operator, on going into the boat, carries on his back a strongly-made knapsack filled with chemicals. Attached to the knapsack is a tube which passes over the operator's head into his mouth, and through which he breathes, the air being kept pure by the chemicals.*

The breathing system was originally designed for rescuing people trapped in mines or from poisonous atmospheres, as reported by the Manchester Courier:

> '*...by constructing a diving dress with which he has lived underwater without any air-tubes connected with the surface, and also a 'pneumatophore' with which he has lived in chambers filled with sulphur fumes and poisonous gases as long as he wished to do so.*'

The description in the journal *The Engineer* suggested that only one of the crew wore the Pneumatophore but this is unlikely if the air inside the boat would only be breathable for just 90 minutes:

> '*One man in the conning tower had the secret breathing apparatus in use, the air of the boat was kept in a fit state for the other men to look after the management of the machinery*'.

The later description in the journal Marine Engineer from January 1880 suggests that all the crew now wore helmets for the breathing apparatus:

> '*The crew, consisting of three, the captain, engineer and owner wear helmets, into which the oxygen is pumped. It is said that when these helmets are removed for a time, a heavy*

drousiness (sic) overcomes the inmates, but upon again being donned, the spirits revive, and the wearer becoms (sic) energetic and alive to the situation.'

Bearing in mind the small volume of air inside the boat and how quickly that air would become foul from even a small leak from the furnace, it is likely that all the crew would need the breathing apparatus after only a short interval with the conning tower hatch closed.

After the loss of the *Resurgam*, Garrett adapted the Pneumatophore into a self-contained diving system which he demonstrated in May 1880 in the river Seine near Levallois:

'Clothed in his diving dress, and furnished with his respiratory apparatus, Mr Garrett first remained for 20 minutes and then for three-quarters of an hour, under the water.'

The man credited with the development of the first closed circuit breathing apparatus was Henry A. Fleuss. Fleuss developed his rebreather system in 1878 for work under water or in poisonous atmospheres; it was designed in association with Siebe, Gorman & Co. and was used at the Seaham Colliery disaster in 1880 and in the flooded Severn Tunnel in 1882.

In March 1880, just after the *Resurgam* was lost, the Marine Engineer reported that Fleuss could be seen at the Polytechnic on Regent Street in London:

'A Mr Fleuss there dons a diving dress and helmet, which enables him to descend into the water, and remain there for some hours, without any connection by air tubes to the surface whatsoever.'

Garrett developed the Pneumatophore before developing his two submarines but we do not know precisely when it was first used, so it is possible that he made a working rebreather before Fleuss. However, the demonstrations in France did not generate any orders for this new breathing system and no prototypes are known to have survived. Garrett did not patent the Pneumatophore and kept the design a secret so we do not have any specifications or drawings for the breathing system. The Pneumatophore may be the first closed circuit rebreather diving system constructed and successfully demonstrated but without models or designs this early rebreather has been lost to history. The one place that a Pneumatophore may still be found is inside the *Resurgam* submarine - the breathing systems the crew used on the journey from Rhyl may have been left behind when the three adventurers left the boat for the last time.

Environment

Resurgam used stored energy in the boiler to drive the steam engine when it was underwater as this was the basic principle of the Lamm 'fireless' engine fitted inside the boat. When underwater the boiler furnace would be damped down and sealed so no air was being used for combustion, but what little air there was inside the boat after the fire was damped would be a hot and rather nasty mixture containing leaking combustion fumes and oil vapour. Having the boiler inside the hull created a humid and uncomfortable environment in the boat, the engineer George Price complained that *'the heat from the boiler was intense, varying from 110-115 degrees'* (43° – 46° C).

The crew would be wearing their Pneumatophore helmets so they were able to breathe but the helmets would make their heads hotter so overheating would soon be a problem, causing headaches, confusion and lethargy in the crew. Dehydration would also be likely; drinking water would be difficult wearing a Pneumatophore helmet yet taking off the helmet to rehydrate would expose the wearer to the hot and poisonous atmosphere.

The submarine would have been very dark inside with just the dim glow of a few decklights providing illumination on the surface, and with what little could penetrate the poor underwater visibility of the Irish Sea when submerged. Candles could have been used to provide light but these would have used up the limited supply of oxygen inside the hull and would add more foul gases to the crew's breathing mix. The submarine may have been lit on the inside by electricity; there is no mention of it in the original design documents but electric lights were said to have been fitted to Garrett's first submarine. The metal cones that formed the ends of the pressure hull were bathed in cold seawater on the outside so water vapour from the steam engine would rapidly condense on the inside of the hull, pooling in the bilge where it would need to be pumped overboard using the bilge pump.

To the discomforts of the crew we can also add seasickness from the foul air, the excessive heat, disorientation in the dark and damp from water condensing on every cold surface. The design of the submarine hints that she would roll and pitch quite easily, even with the two side-mounted hydroplanes acting like yacht bilge keels limiting roll. The crew would also have to contend with the disorientation of wearing breathing apparatus while stuck inside a dark tube with no windows that was being tossed around by the waves - if that did not make them seasick then nothing would. Everything they touched would be wet, some parts of the submarine would be as cold as the sea while others would be boiling hot. Machinery would be sliding or rotating, eager to trap fingers or bang heads, so grabbing a handhold in the dark to maintain balance would be an extremely hazardous undertaking. For the crew in the hull there was nowhere to stand up straight and nowhere to sit. The 2 ft (0.3 m) gap between the top of the boiler lagging and the top of the pressure hull may have provided a place to lay, but not if the boiler was hot as the thin wood lagging was not that effective and it would have roasted whoever tried to lay down. I expect the crew found a way to jam themselves in whatever space they could find between the machinery and the hull and simply put up with the utter misery of it all.

Dynamics and Diving

Resurgam was designed to be slightly positively buoyant but with the minimum of reserve buoyancy, only enough to support the conning tower and the fairing so both remained above the surface of the water when the vehicle was stationary. This submarine was unusual because it did not have ballast tanks that could be flooded to reduce buoyancy for diving or emptied to gain buoyancy on the surface. The *Resurgam* always maintained a small amount of buoyancy so to dive she had to be driven underwater; the engine would drive the vessel forwards, the hydroplanes on the sides of the hull would be angled downwards and the resulting down thrust would push the submarine beneath the surface. This submarine could only submerge if she was moving forwards so if the engine stopped underwater then the boat would simply float back up. This feature was designed to make the vessel safer to operate as it would tend to head back to the safety of the surface if the engine failed.

To be able to submerge in this fashion requires a careful balance of forces. Diving can only be achieved with sufficient speed or sufficiently large hydroplanes, but larger hydroplanes increase drag which then requires more thrust and a larger engine to overcome it. Increasing the angle on the hydroplanes will increase the thrust downwards but also at the expense of increasing the drag. Given a big enough engine and plenty of forward thrust the submarine could be driven underwater, but this would be difficult to achieve for *Resurgam* as she only had a limited amount of forward thrust available. The hydroplanes would act like wings so there would be a maximum angle at which the hydroplanes would be effective. Increasing the angle beyond this value would slow the submarine too much, the boat would 'stall' and float back to the surface. How fast the submarine could really go on the surface or submerged is unknown. In December of 1879 Garrett told the press that the submarine could do 8 to 10 knots, which seems optimistic for a vessel that weighs 30 tons with just 6hp to drive it through the sea. One of the most significant factors that govern submarine speed is the frontal area so the later decision to widen the hull with timber cladding would only have slowed her still further. A more realistic estimate of her speed would be just 2 to 3 knots.

The reserve buoyancy required to support the fairing when the submarine was afloat and fully loaded has been calculated to be 260kg. This assumes that the entire fairing is supported above the waterline. However, Garrett may have reduced the reserve so less of the fairing was out of the water and there was less buoyancy for the hydroplanes to overcome. If the reserve buoyancy was reduced then the submarine would sink down to a level where the buoyancy could support a smaller proportion of the fairing. For example, if the reserve buoyancy was reduced by half then only the upper half of the fairing would remain out of the water. The forward speed required to overcome a full reserve buoyancy of 260kg and half reserve buoyancy of 130kg is given below:

Reserve buoyancy	260kg	130kg
Hydroplane angle		
10°	9.1 kt	6.5 kt
20°	6.5 kt	4.6 kt
30°	5.4 kt	3.8 kt
40°	4.8 kt	3.4 kt

The estimate of the down force that could be produced by the two hydroplanes was calculated by Gary Gardner at MSubs Ltd.

At the full reserve buoyancy and at a shallow hydroplane angle of 10° the submarine would need to be moving forwards at 9.3kt to completely submerge. At a steep angle of 40° the boat would still need to be moving at 4.4kt to submerge, with the engine pushing the 30 ton hull through the water and overcoming the increased drag of the hydroplanes maintained at the steep angle. Even if the reserve buoyancy were reduced by half the submarine would still only dive when the hydroplane angle was a steep 40°. These calculations suggest that with an estimated actual speed of only 2 to 3 knots it is unlikely that *Resurgam* could ever truly dive and propel herself underwater.

It is also not clear why Garrett abandoned the use of ballast tanks, choosing instead to have minimal reserve buoyancy and to drive *Resurgam* beneath the surface using centre-mounted hydroplanes. Ballast tanks were a common feature of all the previous submarines he would have known about as were the stern-mounted hydroplanes he adopted. Garrett's prototype submarine included ballast tanks that could be flooded and pumped dry yet the feature was not then used in *Resurgam*.

Choosing not to include ballast tanks meant that the calculations for the vessel hydrodynamics, weight and balance and propulsion system all had to be correct as the submarine was reliant on a combination of these factors to allow it to submerge. *Resurgam* would not dive if the hull had more drag resistance than had been calculated, if the hydroplanes were less effective, if the submarine was too heavy or if the forward speed was too slow. Ballast tanks would have compensated for a range of possible errors in these calculations so choosing not to include the tanks appears to be a fundamental mistake. The ballast tanks were probably omitted because of limited space inside the pressure hull. The cylindrical hull appears to have been designed around a boiler of sufficient size so adding ballast tanks would require making the hull diameter much larger if the tanks were fitted around the keel or the hull would need to be much longer if the tanks were fitted in the bow and stern. Making the hull wider or longer brings an additional range of problems that perhaps Garrett wished to avoid. Unfortunately the thoughts that led to this design decision were not recorded or not preserved for posterity.

The predicted endurance of the submarine was only 4 hours at a speed of 2-3 knots, a total operating range of some 4-5 miles allowing for time to attack a target. In this time the submarine would have to head towards its target underwater from some secure location, locate the target, loose off a torpedo then head back to safety. Some obvious difficulties with this plan immediately spring to mind: If the submarine stopped it would float to the surface, so the attack run would have to be done at sufficient speed to keep the boat underwater

- The boat could not raise steam quickly so if the stored water ran out then the boat would stop, float up and be a sitting duck on the surface
- If the *Resurgam* fired a Mk 1 Whitehead torpedo she would immediately lose 383kg (845 lbs) and become that much lighter, bobbing to the surface at a very inconvenient moment
- As the 2.5 tons of coal she carried was used up, the boat would gain an equivalent amount of buoyancy which would require more forward speed to overcome when submerging
- There is no mention of a compass for navigation and how well it would work inside an iron hull is open to question

The First and Last Voyage

The events surrounding the loss of the *Resurgam* are not well understood. Garrett was never forthcoming about what occurred on the day that the submarine was lost and the only witness to speak about it, engineer Price, told his version 45 years after the event when the memories would have been much faded. The story of her loss starts at 2.30 p.m. on 26 November 1879. Before a small crowd of journalists, shipyard workers and members of the Garrett family, the *Resurgam* submarine was lowered by crane into the Great Float in Birkenhead near Liverpool (Figure 18). The Great Float is a natural tidal inlet formed into two large docks called the East Float and the West Float, which divide the towns of Birkenhead and Wallasey. Among other things, during the test Garrett learned that the boiler would cause the temperature of the boat to rise uncomfortably when closed down with the main hatch shut.

Resurgam was recovered from the water shortly after this trial and then replaced into the Great Float on the 10th December 1879, in preparation for the first voyage. Garrett had argued with Cochran against taking *Resurgam* overland for the Admiralty trials in Portsmouth and it was an argument that Garrett won, despite the obvious

Figure 18: Resurgam at Birkenhead just before launching, with Jackson (fwd), Price (aft) and Garrett holding his two year old daughter Georgina

problems of a long sea voyage in an untried submarine in the middle of winter. Garrett, the engineer George Price and Captain W.E. Jackson left Birkenhead at 9pm and steamed off into a dark and misty night, which immediately raises questions about their judgement over seamanship matters.

Garrett reported that the weather was so thick that in order to navigate Jackson needed to stay outside the conning tower while Garrett steered. This raises a number of questions, in particular how Jackson managed to hang on to the outside the submarine if she was ballasted down for diving and underway with waves breaking over her? The plan called for the crew to perform tests within an area out at sea called the Victoria Deep, however fog the following day prevented this and instead they *'moved about testing various parts of our machinery till the next morning'*. The weather the following day cleared up allowing more tests to be completed. The vessel had been at sea for more than 30 hours, Garrett later commenting that a *'great part of this time we were under water'*. As has been noted by Bowers, this is an unlikely scenario and it was probably just Garrett self-aggrandising for the press release. The duration of the latent energy in the steam reservoir would have been around 4 hours. During this time it would have been possible that the submarine was submerged, however when its stored energy was depleted the boat needed a few days to bring the boiler back up to temperature. George Price, recalling the journey in the mid-1920's, claimed similarly that the vessel managed to submerge to a depth of 30-40 feet for more than 30 hours, also noting that the heat from the boiler was intense and that a problem with the air pressure caused discomfort on the ear drums.

The crew eventually arrived at Rhyl exhausted from their journey and needing to make repairs to the boat after the failure of several minor parts and to change the propeller (Figure 19). Garrett arranged for work to be done at a foundry in nearby Rhuddlan where the parts could be fabricated before being fitted by the three submariners. When he arrived in Rhyl, Garrett announced to the newspapers that: *'We remain at Rhyl for a few days, to perfect a few little matters of some importance to our future comfort.'* But despite the suggestion of a short stay, a combination of bad weather and mechanical repairs kept the boat in Rhyl throughout the whole of December and most of January.

Garrett maintained communications with the media despite being stuck in Rhyl. On 3rd January the Manchester Courier reported another trial held just before Christmas where *Resurgam* was tested in the River Voryd, with the gallant submariners seeing how the boat handled in shallow water. Garrett also took the time to announce that the submarine was ready to resume her trip to Portsmouth but he dare not leave as the weather had been windy and the sea far too rough:

'It has not been a gale, but a hurricane, the Resurgam would be quite safe out at sea, but we dare not at present attempt to take her through the miles of breakers and shallow water that are off this coast'.

After two months sitting in a tiny Welsh harbour Garrett decided to continue the journey to Portsmouth, but this time the submarine would have an escort vessel as Garrett had previously returned to Liverpool and purchased the steam yacht Elphin. The Rhyl Journal reported that Resurgam finally resumed her journey down the coast to Portsmouth at 10pm on Tuesday 24th February 1880, just before high tide, motoring along on the surface under her own steam in the company of Elphin.

What was happening with the weather at that time is also uncertain but it is central to the story of her loss. Murphy says that the weather deteriorated after the two vessels had left Rhyl, rising to a west-north-west gale late on Wednesday night (25th), nearly 24 hours after the pair had sailed. But on Monday 23rd the Meteorological Office forecast light to moderate northerly winds for North Wales and on Tuesday it predicted light to moderate south westerly winds, fair but unsettled. The gale was not forecast until Thursday 26th, with strong to gale force winds with cold showers. Price reported that *Elphin* developed engine trouble at a point in their journey Garrett described as 'off the Great Ormes Head' (Figure 20), so the crew of the *Resurgam* were called to aid the support vessel. There is some confusion over dates as Bowers states that the engine problem happened early on Wednesday morning, only 12 hours after they had sailed. The submarine was brought under tow with a line attached from the stern of the *Elphin* to the tow point on the leading edge of the conning tower fairing. The crew took all of their belongings with them to the yacht; Jackson even remembered to take the submarine's pennant. While the submarine crew were still on *Elphin* effecting repairs, Price said that the weather increased to a full gale leaving the crew unable to return:

> 'During that time a gale sprang up, and prevented us from returning to the submarine. We towed her until ten o' clock the following morning, when she broke her hawser, and consequently we lost her'.

Figure 19: Rhyl harbour in 1997

What happened next is not clear; one suggestion is that waves breaking over the low hull sent water down the conning tower as the main hatch could not be sealed from the outside. *Resurgam* took on water, the towing hawser broke under the additional weight of the submarine and she disappeared beneath the waves at 10 am on Wednesday 25th or Thursday 26th February 1880 depending on which story you believe. The Rhyl Record on 28th February noted that *Resurgam*

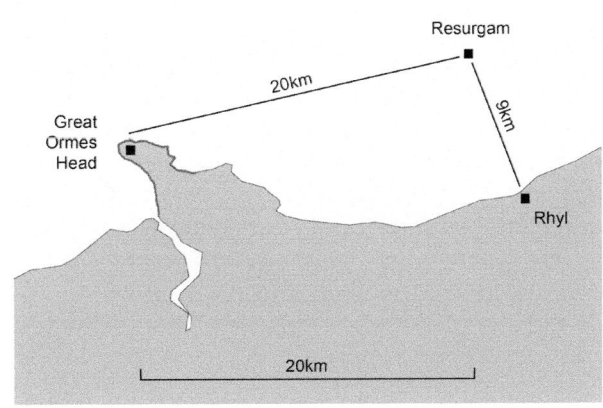

Figure 20: Chart showing the location of the wreck in relation to Rhyl and Great Ormes Head

and *Elphin* did not reach Holyhead as expected and that a yacht resembling *Elphin* was seen heading east towards Liverpool without the *Resurgam*. This was reported to have happened on Wednesday 25th so it is likely that *Resurgam* was lost that day, rather than on the Thursday.

Resurgam sank at a location recorded by Garrett as 'somewhere off Great Ormes Head', when in fact she was much closer to Rhyl having only managed to make her way a few miles offshore. The submarine left Rhyl at 10pm on Tuesday 24th and was reported by Price to have sunk at 10am on Wednesday 26th, yet in all that time the submarine and escort had not made any real progress westwards and were only 9km north of where they had started.

The weather forecast for North Wales published by the Meteorological Office in February 1880:

Monday 23rd	Northerly winds, fresh at Holyhead but light to moderate elsewhere
Tuesday 24th	Light to moderate south westerly winds, fair but unsettled
Wednesday 25th	North westerly breezes, moderate to fresh, cloudy, cold showers, changeable
Thursday 26th	North westerly winds, strong to gale force with cold showers
Friday 27th	Westerly to northerly winds, moderate to strong with cold rain or snow

The foul weather was cause for *Elphin* to run further east for the shelter of the river Dee and the port of Mostyn. Price goes on to say that *Elphin* was lost the following day after parting her chains and running ashore. The paddle tug *Iron King* was signalled to come to the assistance of the stranded steam yacht but it only succeeded in ramming and sinking her. Garrett attempted to organise a search for *Resurgam* when the weather improved but the submarine was never seen again by anyone, including the shareholders and directors of the Garrett Submarine Boat and Pneumatophore Company. Although the vessel was the company's primary tangible asset, its loss was not widely advertised and shares in the company continued to be sold at least six months after the catastrophe.

Searching for *Resurgam*

Nothing more was heard about *Resurgam* after she sank as Garrett had lost his only asset and the press had lost interest. England's first mechanically powered submarine was forgotten until 1922 when the nautical magazine called Sea Breezes published a short article describing her development and her loss.[9] This article prompted a yachtsman to write a letter to the magazine stating that about thirty years earlier, while sailing his yacht from the island of Anglesey in the direction of Liverpool, close to the harbour of Rhyl at a very low spring tide, he collided with what he described as a *'rusty cylindrical object of considerable size'*. Enquiries made by the article's author disclosed that the correspondent who had collided with the rusty cylindrical object was a very credible person indeed, in fact a senior member of the editorial board of the magazine. Spurred on by this apparent clue, in 1975 the article's author invited Dr. E. T. Hall, director of the Laboratory for Archaeology at Oxford University, to undertake a proton magnetometer survey of an area to the west of the entrance of Rhyl harbour, an area local fisherman identified as foul ground, in the hope of detecting the rusty object. The quest was aided by shipwreck explorer Syd Wignall along with John Stubbs and other members of the Gwynedd branch of the Welsh Association of Sub-Aqua Clubs. The submarine was not found and Dr. Hall formed the opinion that no ferrous objects of the size of the *Resurgam* lay in that area.[10] Commander R. Compton-Hall from the Royal Navy Submarine Museum also organised a search prior to 1981 but again found nothing.

The University College of North Wales in conjunction with the Welsh Institute of Maritime Archaeology and History started the Resurgam Project in 1981 with the intention of locating the submarine.[11] The Royal Navy completed another search in 1981 but again without finding anything. The Royal Navy Submarine Museum organised a third search in 1983 but this was aborted due to bad weather and this was followed by another search 1985. In August 1987, Marine Archaeological Survey (MAS) conducted a search close inshore to the west of Rhyl towards Colwyn Bay using a proton magnetometer and side scan sonar but this was aborted when they grounded the survey boat in shallow water.[12] Another search was conducted in 1988 by an unknown group. Bill Garrett and Richard Bufton's expedition in the summer of 1989 was centred north of Puffin Island, west of the Conwy estuary and north-east of the Great Orme, but found nothing as did two other Garrett funded searches in 1992 and 1993.[13]

It is not surprising that the many surveys could not find Resurgam as they were all looking in the wrong place. The chosen search area was based on information given by Price, the engineer on board *Resurgam*, in a newspaper article written 45 years after the submarine was lost.[14] As we shall see, what was found on the seabed is often at odds with the story that Price related to the press.

---

[9] Sea Breezes 1922
[10] Wignall 1978
[11] UCNW 1981
[12] Garrett, pers. comm., Redknap, pers. comm.
[13] Garrett, pers. comm., Newell 1996
[14] Liverpool Echo 1925, 8 Dec

Pipe Route Survey

In September 1992 a pipeline route survey was completed by Costain for the Hamilton Oil Company Ltd. which covered the area where the *Resurgam* lay (Figure 21). The survey was done prior to laying a 33.5km gas pipeline from the Douglas Complex 15 miles (24 km) from the Welsh coast to a processing plant at Point of Ayr in North Wales. The contract to lay the pipe was awarded to McDermott-ETPM in 1993 and they used lay barge DLB1601 to complete the job in 1995.[15] The submarine was not discovered during the route survey but a scour line on the seabed running 116° / 296° T was marked which may have been associated with the wreck. This work is significant for two reasons: firstly because the submarine was not detected on the route survey and secondly the vessels operating around the pipelay operation may be the cause for the wreck to have been unearthed from the seabed.

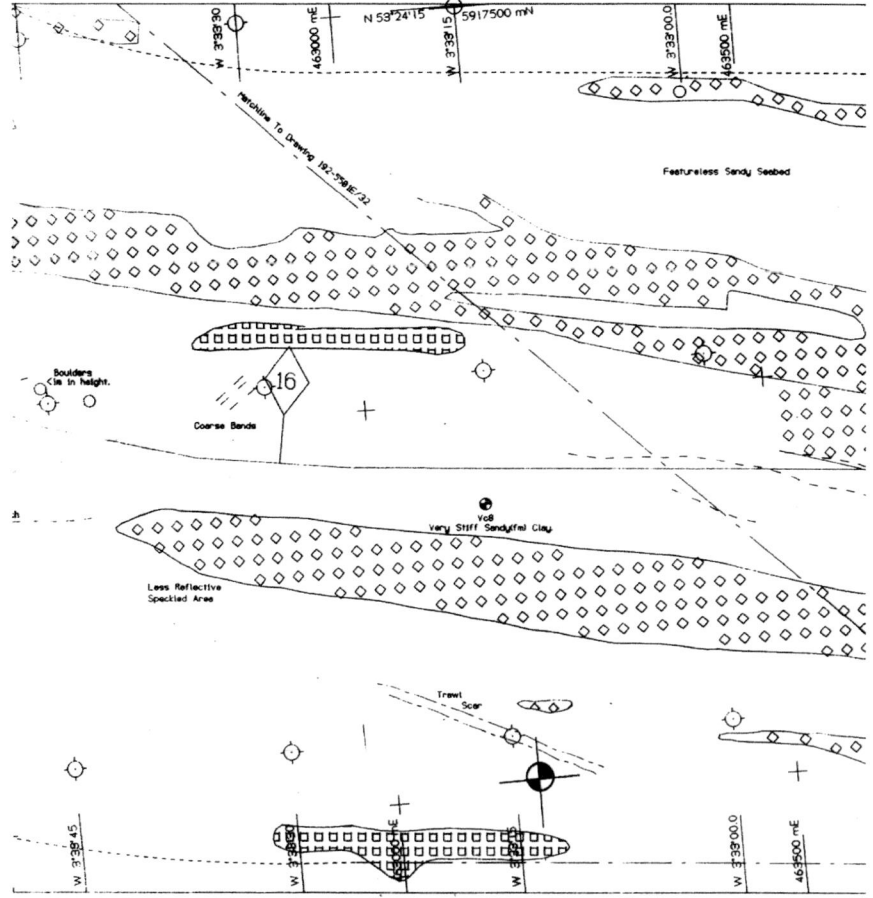

Figure 21: Detail from the 1:5000 scale plan of the pipe route survey (Courtesy of Costain Ltd.)

---

[15] Oil and Gas Journal 1995

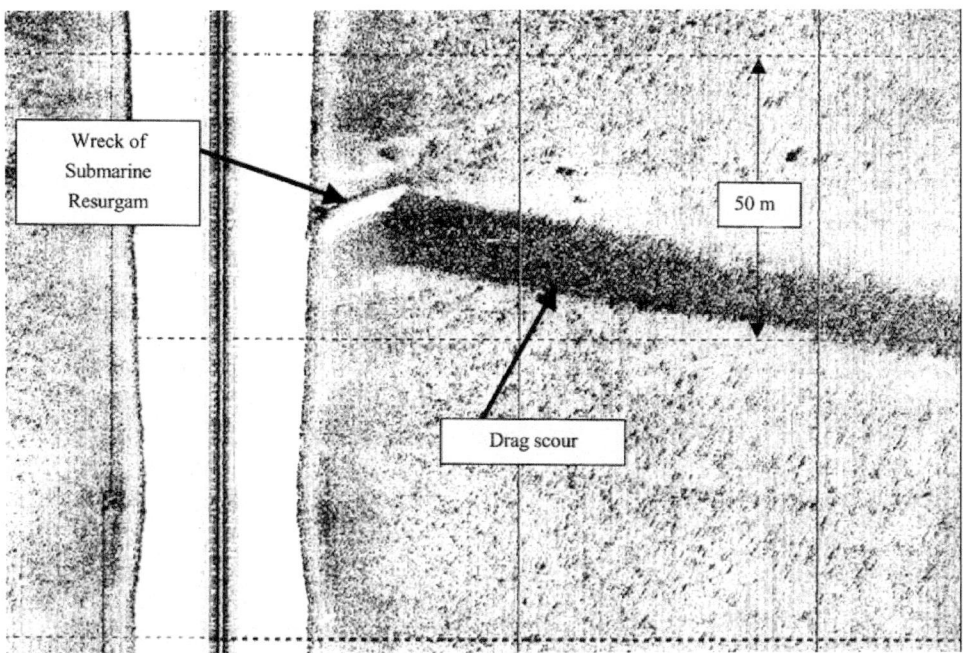

Figure 22: Side scan sonar image of the submarine and associated scour (BHP Billiton)

A side scan sonar image from a BHP Billiton presentation was found in the project archive but the source and date of the image are unknown (Figure 22). The image shown above is the original version with the submarine hull lying on her starboard side which suggests a run direction 212° T. However, the 50 m grid spacing label is incorrect and should be 30 m as the submarine is 12 m long. The noticeable dark scour line is shown heading away from the top of the hull in a direction 314°T but the direction of the scour is wrong so the picture may be a mirror image that needs to be flipped upside down to be viewed correctly.

Rediscovery

In October 1995, Dennis Hunt, the owner of a small Conwy trawler called *Patricia Dee*, fouled his nets on the seabed off Rhyl in North Wales.[16] Keith Hurley, a diver from nearby Chester was called in as regularly cleared nets from obstructions for local fishermen. Hurley had been involved in previous searches for the *Resurgam* so he was familiar with her distinctive shape so once he was in underwater he was able to immediately identify the *Resurgam* under the snagged trawl net. The finders notified the media and a major TV news company filmed the wreck and filmed people on the boat while they were over the site. Those invited on board that day later reported that the fishing boat's navigational instruments had tape placed over the displays, presumably to hide the position co-ordinates of the wreck from visitors. The Archaeological Diving Unit (ADU) working for H.M. Government (and therefore Cadw: Welsh Historic Monuments when in Welsh waters) contacted the finder and it was agreed that an assessment would be made with a view to designation under the Protection of Wrecks Act 1973.

However, when the ADU arrived with boat and equipment on 12th April 1996, the finders refused to divulge the position without being paid first. William 'Bill' Garrett, great grandson to Rev. W. Garrett, offered them £4,000 as a starting bid, but the finders declined as they were hoping for a £40,000 to £50,000 settlement.[17] Bill Garrett flew over from the US and arrived the following day with his daughter so he could help the ADU with the assessment. Bill, a New Jersey businessman, had organised and funded a number of previous searches for the *Resurgam* and had also brought together the family's archive of George's papers. Further attempts by Bill and others to persuade the finders to co-operate failed so it was decided to view the TV footage recorded over the site to see if there were clues about the wreck's position. Using a TV editing suite in Liverpool, the video was studied by the ADU and a sketch made of coastal features in an attempt to identify them. This information was used to draw transect lines on Admiralty charts to allow a tentative position to be plotted which was off the entrance to the river Dee.

The ADU's boat *Xanadu* was moved to the port of Mostyn, 17 miles to the west of Rhyl, but there followed a period of bad weather and the ADU were only able to reach the site on 15th April. This opportunity was used to undertake a magnetometer and echo sounder search of the wreck's deduced position; unfortunately the coastline was not visible due to the bad weather and no significant anomalies were detected. Bill Garrett and his daughter decided to return to the USA and when the weather cleared on the 19th, *Xanadu* made passage for the ADU's next port of call which was Holyhead. In clearer conditions with the shore visible, the boat passed close to the plotted location and the crew realised that key topographic features on the shore had been misidentified. They were able to realign transects and a new position further offshore was indicated. Following the line of one very clear alignment of coastal features, an

---

[16] Newell 1996, Gorton 1996
[17] Gorton 1996b

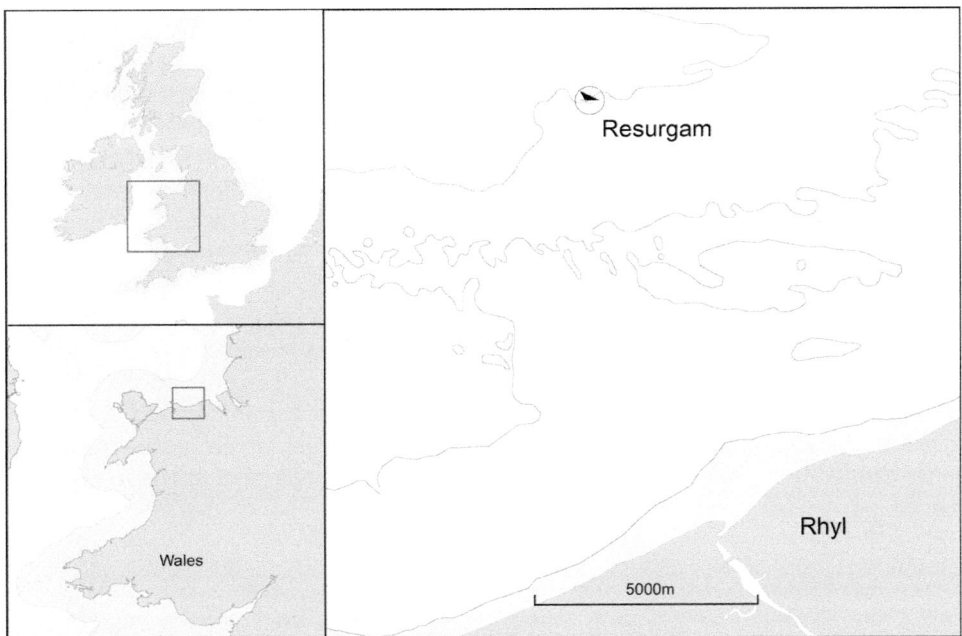

Figure 23: Resurgam wreck site location off North Wales

uncharted wreck of approximately the right characteristics as *Resurgam* was located. Knowing the vulnerability of the wreck, the ADU suggested in their report of April 1996 to the Advisory Committee on Historic Wreck Sites[18] that the best solution would be to move *Resurgam* to a place of safety to prevent damage.

Bill Garrett had been to the UK many times in pursuit of his forebear's submarine and decided that he would fly back to Wales with specialists in locating objects on the seabed. In mid-June 1996 he and John Perry Fish of American Underwater Search and Survey arrived, together with the Plymouth-based research vessel *Terschelling* that was to be used as a base for operations. The ADU rearranged its schedule to be present and with the second pass of the side scan sonar deployed from *Xanadu*, the readily identifiable image of *Resurgam* was revealed at the location of the uncharted wreck. The wreck lay approximately 9km from the coast and directly off the town of Rhyl (Figure 23).

Using the ADU's diving system and *Terschelling's* Hyball remotely operated vehicle, observations were made which confirmed that the submarine was in reasonable condition, with some of the wooden cladding around the central section of the hull still in place. The hull was leaning over to starboard and a large dent could be seen in the top of the conning tower (Figure 24). There were also two holes in the iron hull toward the bow and the propeller blades, conning-tower hatch, rudder and hydroplanes were missing. The team from the *Terschelling* under the direction of the ship's owner, Capt.

---
[18] ADU 1996

Nigel Boston, sealed the conning tower opening and the larger hole in the bow; these were covered with steel plates clamped in place to deter unauthorised access. As there were no resources to move *Resurgam* quickly to a place of safety, a recommendation was made by the ADU to Cadw and the Advisory Committee that the site would benefit from legal protection and, twelve days later on 6th July, 1996, she was designated under the Protection of Wrecks Act 1973 (SI 1996/1741). The ADU returned to the site two days after it was designated and found that the steel plates used to seal off access to the submarine had been removed and there was obvious damage to the wreck. Two portholes that had remained in-situ in the conning tower had been forcibly removed, the mechanism for closing the exhaust vent had been sawn off and the cast iron steering wheel in the conning tower had been shattered with parts dropped on the seabed nearby. Reports suggested that two groups of people, including one known to the ADU, had dived on the site in the few days up to and possibly immediately after it was designated. A request to the diving community to return items anonymously resulted in one of the portholes being handed in to the Liverpool Coastguard and another returned to the site during the SubMap project the following year.

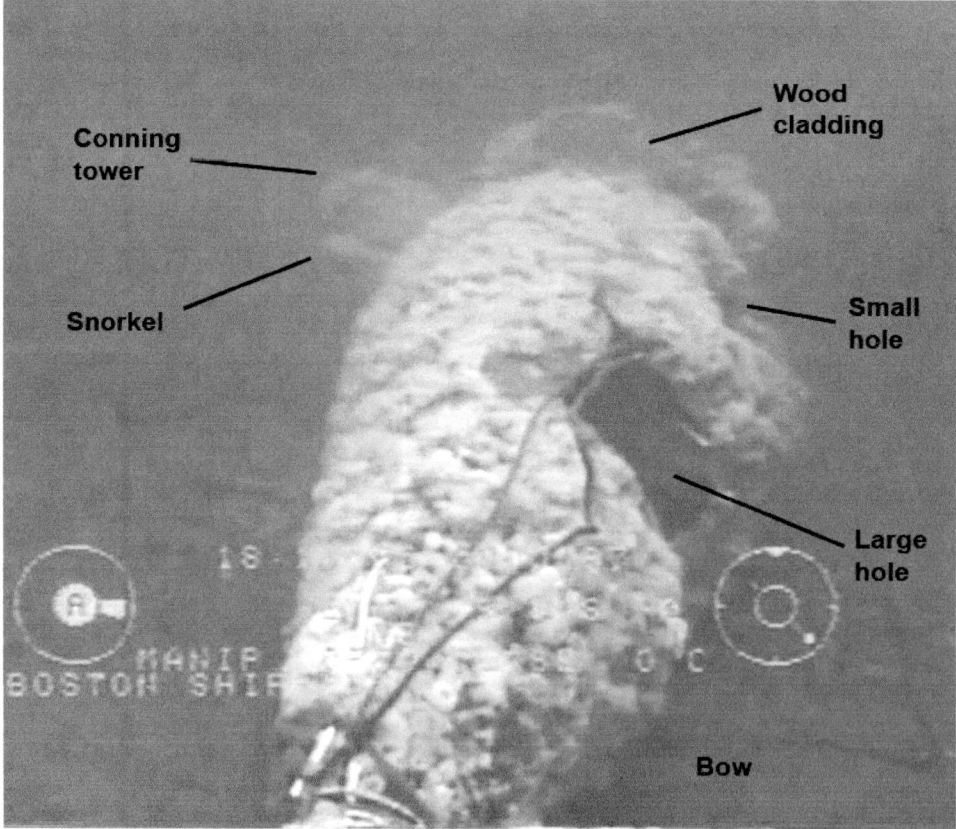

Figure 24: Resurgam as she was seen in 1997 lying hard over on her starboard side, view from the bow towards the stern taken from ROV video footage

The *SubMap* Project

Introduction

In order to keep the local population informed about the events surrounding this historically important wreck, Cadw: Welsh Historic Monuments organised a public meeting in Rhyl in December 1996. The interest and enthusiasm shown by both the public and the diving community lead to a decision by the ADU to organise an archaeological recording project that would be open to sport divers. The project, called *SubMap,* was designed to give sport divers the opportunity to be involved in the investigation of an important designated historic wreck, and so help promote a sympathetic approach to archaeological sites underwater. The survey work was undertaken from 4th June 1997 until 15th June 1997 with the survey plan based on the requirements of the SubMap Proposals[19], the SubMap Project Design[20] and the Preliminary Research Design.[21] Most of what we know about the condition of the *Resurgam* is from work done during the 1997 SubMap project which ran from 4th to 15th June 1997. SubMap was a multi-disciplinary study of the site undertaken by a mixed group of professional and amateur organisations. The scope of the project included:

Phase 1

- Survey the hull exterior
- Locate, investigate and record of all material on the seabed around the wreck
- Measure the corrosion potential of the iron hull and attach of sacrificial anodes
- Complete a biological survey of the wreck and its environs
- Record then remove the marine life on the hull prior to detailed hull recording
- Train divers in a range of techniques applicable to archaeological investigations

Phase 2

- Excavate any sediments to allow identification of objects in the debris field
- Move any object associated with the submarine to a holding area adjacent to the wreck

This phase required the authorisation of limited excavation under license from Cadw.

Phase 3

- Excavate sediments from within the hull
- Record the interior of the hull

---

[19] ADU 1996
[20] ADU 1996
[21] Newell 1996

Volunteer project participation was mostly invited through the Nautical Archaeology Society (NAS) although the original finders of the submarine were contacted directly. Divers and non-divers were invited to attend for anything from a quick visit to dive on the wreck to participation during the full two weeks of the project. NAS training courses were offered in a range of subjects including basic surveying, use of survey software, sonar imaging and marine life identification.

Through the goodwill of Boston Shipping, *SubMap* was fortunate to have the services again of the research vessel *Terschelling* as project support ship and the base for operations at sea. In addition, an inflatable boat provided by Northern Divers acted as a link to shore together with numerous small boats provided by NAS participants. The project was also fortunate in that Sonardyne International used the site as an opportunity to help develop their RovTrak acoustic positioning system, while Hamish Forbes of Seatronics brought along an Imagenex sector scanning sonar which was briefly used for diver monitoring.

Rhyl Yacht Club made their club house and all its facilities available to the project as a shore base including their showers and boat slipway which were essential for the volunteer diving operations. As the harbour at Rhyl is tidally constrained, these facilities made it easier for teams of divers in small boats to leave on the falling tide, dive during low-water slack and then return to the harbour on the rising tide. The shore side arrangements were managed by Garry Momber from the NAS training office, with a radio links to the vessels offshore organised by NAS member Robin Witheridge. This communication system worked smoothly and allowed tasks to be allocated to divers before they left the harbour. David Gregory of the National Museum of Denmark's Centre for Maritime Archaeology undertook a series of measurements of surface pH and corrosion potential on the iron hull during the project. Dr Gregory's investigation[22] highlighted the need for cathodic protection to help protect the wreck and, during the project, the first of a series of replacement zinc anodes were attached to the hull at key points in the second week.

An excavation license was granted by Cadw to Alex Hildred, visiting archaeologist from the Mary Rose Trust, which allowed excavation of selected areas within the debris field around the wreck and allowed for the removal, recording and reburial of any artefacts found on the site. The excavation was undertaken using a small team of volunteers based on *Terschelling* with an area 8 metres south of the submarine designated as being the priority for excavation during the first assessment in 1996. Visible structural features on the seabed included two iron straps and in 1996 these appeared to be connected by a metal plate. It was assumed that these had been retaining straps for the wooden cladding that covered the submarine and might still be attached to the missing portions of the cladding, thereby marking the original burial position of the hull.

SubMap was successful on a number of levels. Even though the wreck is small and diving was only possible for less than two hours during daylight because of tidal constraints,

---

[22] Gregory 2000

more than one hundred and ten people were actively involved during the two weeks of the project, ninety four were sport divers and the majority were from Wales. The 10 m underwater visibility was unusually good for the time as less than 1 m is normal on the site in June and the weather was also reasonable for most of the project.

SubMap Methods

The primary Phase 1 aims for the survey team was the location, investigation and recording of all material on the seabed around the wreck. To achieve these aims a number of objectives had to be completed:

- Create a survey plan
- Establish the position and orientation of the hull within a real-world co-ordinate frame
- Record the position of all detectable targets within a distance of 50 m from the hull
- Produce a plan of the site showing the submarine and associated targets
- Record all survey and positioning information to be available for later reprocessing
- Produce a report on the process and the results of the survey

Previous work on site had identified that *Resurgam* lay exposed on the seabed with her starboard side partially buried and with her bows pointing to the west. A large proportion of the wood cladding that was around the hull was missing, as were the conning tower hatch, rudders and port hydroplane and there was also some impact damage to the conning tower on the port side aft (Figure 25).

Divers had visited the site and removed some parts of the hull and fittings but it was not known whether these missing parts were deposited around the site or had been recovered. The search tasks were planned to look for the smallest targets detectable with the instruments being used. The seabed around the submarine was composed of a gravel substrate covered by a flat layer of mobile sediment that was no more than 150 mm thick, so it was initially assumed that the targets should be visible on the surface or only just buried. The hull was the only target of that size within 500 m and would show up clearly on a remote sensing survey. Gas pipelines lie to the north of the site and the pipes lie well within the historic wreck area in a shallow trench close to the surface.

The DSV *Terschelling* was used for ROV and dive support for the search, survey and excavation operations and the vessel provided a base and accommodation for the survey team and the Archaeological Diving Unit for the duration of the job. The vessel worked well as a permanent diving platform as it was stable, had a large working deck area and heavy lift capability. She could support two divers on surface supplied air and had a recompression chamber on board. The dive supervisor controlled operations from a purpose built control room within the ship that was also used for ROV control so the dive supervisor could use the ROV to monitor the divers underwater. The vessel was fitted with a low pressure air compressor that was used to power the airlift used for

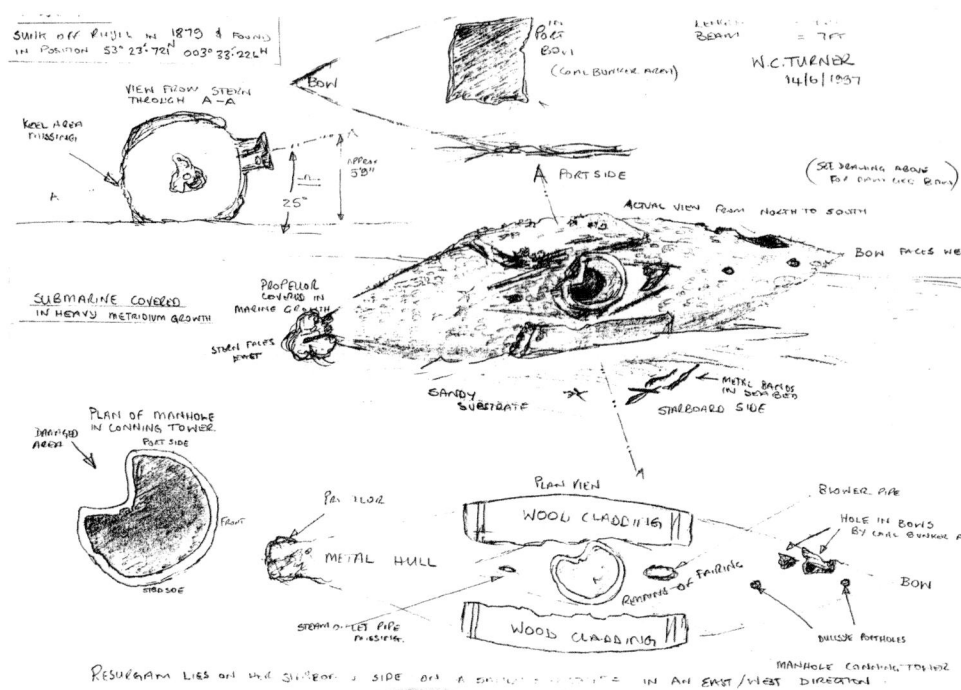

Figure 25: Detailed sketch of the submarine created during SubMap by Bill Turner

excavation of the seabed. The ADU vessel *Xanadu* was used for deploying the array of acoustic beacons and completing the remote sensing survey data collection tasks. For the remainder of the time she was used as the base for ADU diving operations or as a ferry (Figure 26).

The two Remotely Operated Vehicles (ROVs) were rigged together, with a small, free-swimming Hyball inspection ROV carried in a garage on top of a Slingsby crawler ROV. When underwater the Hyball could leave its garage and travel some distance from the crawler, limited only by the length of its tether. The Hyball ROV carried a colour video camera and the images from it were recorded on videotape on the support vessel. The ROVs could operate even when diving operations had stopped because of strong tidal currents; this gave the survey team a much more efficient capability than would have been achieved by divers alone.

Surface positioning was provided by a Trimble DSM Pro GPS (GNSS) receiver using differential corrections from a Scorpio receiver and when used correctly the system could achieve an accuracy of better than 5 m. This instrument was used for the geophysical survey done by the ADU and AUSS and for deployment and calibration of the underwater acoustic positioning system. A Sonardyne ROVTrak underwater Acoustic Positioning System (APS) was used as the primary positioning tool underwater. The system computed positions of a diver or an ROV in three dimensions, in real time, to an

Figure 26: Terschelling moored over the top of the wreck during SubMap

accuracy of better than 50 mm over the whole survey area. The system used standard Long Baseline (LBL) acoustic techniques used by the offshore industry and in other similar systems used in marine archaeology. Sonardyne used the SubMap project as an opportunity to test and develop the underwater tracking system in real conditions around a wreck. ROVTrak was used to guide the crawler ROV around the seabed during seabed searches; it was used to position survey points and features on the wreck and it was used to track divers undertaking metal detector searches around the submarine.

The Imagenex scanning sonar was set up on a pole hammered into the seabed so the sonar could be used for monitoring divers working around the submarine. Although the sonar was useful for monitoring the positions of divers on the site it was soon removed as the cable connecting it to the surface was interfering with the divers' umbilical hoses.

SubMap Geophysical Survey

The ADU divers had previously visited the wreck so it was known that there was some debris around the hull visible on the seabed. During the previous visit to the site in June 1996, a side scan sonar had also been used by AUSS Ltd. to obtain a position for the submarine and to locate any objects on the seafloor. The surface positioning system used for the survey was the GPS standard positioning service and differential corrections were not applied so the position of the submarine was established to an accuracy of approximately ±50 m.[23] The initial side scan survey showed that there were 11 targets around the site (Appendix 1, Table

---

[23] This was a time when selective availability (SA) was still enabled in the GPS system which reduced position accuracy

1, AUSS1 – 11) which were to be investigated during SubMap but the computed positions of the targets that had been located were also only given to an accuracy of ±50 m.[24] Due to the poor position accuracy of the first side scan survey it was necessary to repeat the side scan survey work over the site in an attempt to generate more accurate positions for any visible debris. The aim was to use side scan sonar to detect surface features and use a magnetometer and towed metal detector to find any ferrous objects on or buried just beneath the seabed. A sub-bottom profiler was not to be used on the site as it was thought that the missing parts of the submarine were too small to show up distinctly using this equipment. Detailed bathymetry of the site was not recorded as it had previously been determined from the previous side scan sonar survey in 1996 that the seabed on the site was flat and featureless apart from the noted shallow scour.[25]

The SubMap geophysics data collection was done by the ADU and AUSS Ltd. The geophysics work was to be completed before the large dive vessel *Terschelling* was stationed over the wreck as the large ship and her wide mooring spread would be an obstacle. However, due to problems with the weather the work was delayed and the survey was attempted with *Terschelling* moored over the submarine which unfortunately produced poor quality results. Positioning for the survey vessel was provided by Differential GPS (DGPS) and positions for the towfish computed from the vessel position and towfish layback. Unfortunately the DGPS receiver was not using differential corrections to compute position during data collection and this problem was only detected during post-processing, so the position of the sonar records were of no better precision than the previous survey in 1996. Two side scan sonar instruments were used during the survey, a lower quality Imagenex 858 provided by PP Electronics and a high quality EdgeTech system provided by AUSS. Unfortunately the results from the EdgeTech system were never made available to the survey team by AUSS so the lower quality Imagenex data had to be used for target analysis (Appendix 1, Table 2, CS001-13). The use of a towed Geometrics caesium magnetometer was part of the original survey plan but the magnetometer could not be made to work correctly by AUSS so again no results were provided to the survey team. The Imagenex side scan data was of insufficient quality to be able to produce a sonar mosaic of the seabed around the submarine as the position information from the vessel is questionable and the usual parallel search lines required to create a mosaic were not run.

Operations

The SubMap underwater survey work was done using a combination of enthusiastic sport divers and unpaid professionals. The logistics of this type of operation can be difficult but this job demonstrated that useful results can be achieved. Strong tides and bad weather hampered the job during the first week which meant that some of the planned tasks could not be completed as the project was only to run for two weeks. The vessel was only on site and working for a total of nine days with full operational capability for only six days and underwater visibility on the site varied between approximately 3 m and 10 m. Information collected during the dives was processed on the support vessel as the work progressed so

---

[24] Fish 1996
[25] At this time only low resolution single beam bathymetry was possible as multibeam sonar was not widely available

the next day's work could be planned using the available results so far; this gave the survey team a better indication of the state of the site and allowed work to be scheduled as the project progressed.

It became necessary to separate the work done by the survey team and that done by the sport divers due to the sheer numbers of divers in the water. The project was very well attended, so sometimes it was not possible to undertake recording work on the submarine as there were too many divers on it. The survey team on the support vessel had access to the site whenever it was possible to dive, but the sport divers were limited to times when they could get their boats in the water. It was decided that the slack water period was to be given over to the sport divers and the remainder was available to the survey team. This arrangement worked well as the survey team could be on site just before and just after slack water and the tidal current found at that time was useful for washing away stirred up sediment when excavating. The survey team could also work the opposite tide when the sport divers could not get on site which called for some early morning and late evening dives. The diving was done using a mixture of surface supplied air and SCUBA techniques. All airlift excavation, rigging and heavy work was done using tethered surface supply but the majority of the survey work and searching was done using free-swimming divers using SCUBA equipment. The survey and excavation team on Terschelling completed a total of 67 dives plus 44 ROV dives.[26]

Subsea Positioning

At the start of SubMap the submarine was re-located using coordinates from the 1996 side scan sonar survey. The position of the submarine was confirmed by divers and this was then used to define the survey area centre, the required anchor pattern for the dive support vessel and the locations for the ROVTrak beacons. The site area was a square of 200 m each side, centred on the submarine and oriented to grid north (Appendix 1, Table 3). Many of the SubMap objectives relied on precise positioning underwater and this was done using a combination of acoustic positioning system (APS) and a network of survey control points. The APS could only be used by the survey team so a second set of control points had to be established closer to the submarine for use by the volunteer divers with tape measures. The four acoustic beacons used by the APS were placed in tripods on the seabed by divers; they were located outside the main working area of the site in a square approximately 70 m from the submarine. The beacons were placed as close to the search area as possible while keeping them out of the working area of the crawler ROV. The final computed positions of the subsea beacons were to an accuracy of 0.25 m (95%) (Appendix 1, Table 4); no movement was detected in the beacons during the survey and positions for points taken at the start of the operation correlated within tolerance with positions obtained at the end of the survey. The use of both tape measures and acoustic positioning was necessary because of the size of the site and the numbers of divers who were working there. In addition, the *Resurgam* survey was used as a site for field testing some of the combined site survey methods developed by the survey team during recent work in Plymouth, UK [27] (Figure 27).

---

[26] Hildred, Holt & Boston 1997
[27] Dart et. al. 1996

The volunteer divers needed their own set of survey control points (CPs) to position objects on the seabed and features on the submarine. The points were installed on the seabed then positioned using the ROVTrak APS and tape measurements. The control points were 60 mm diameter aluminium tubes approximately 2 m long, hammered into the seabed until they were securely fixed in place. Plastic hooks 70 mm long were fixed to the bottom of the poles just above seabed level to be used for attaching tape measures. The hooks were placed low down on the poles so any tension on a tape measure hooked to the pole would not make the pole move, but after hammering in the poles were so secure they would not move anyway. Many of these poles are still in place on the site nearly 20 years later.

Figure 27: Diver positioning a survey control point using the ROVTrak acoustic positioning system

Ten control points were installed approximately 5 m from the submarine's hull, with the two points PT and ST included so that bracing could be added to the network of measurements. The bow and stern of the submarine were included in the control network so the position of the submarine within the network could be established at an early stage and also because these two points could be used by the survey team as secondary CPs if required (see Appendix 1 Table 5). The longest tape measurement required to compute the control point positions was only about 15 m, less than the 20 m maximum that should be used. Each of the control points was positioned using the ROVTrak APS. These positions were improved by adding distance measurements made between the survey points and re-computing the positions with the survey program *Site Surveyor*. As the survey work progressed it became necessary to add further control points to cover new areas where the divers were working as the excavation to the south of the submarine was beyond the network of control points. The new control points were added to the secondary network by taking acoustic positions and tape measure baseline measurements then again re-computing the positions of the points in Site Surveyor. Measurements were made between the control points on a number of separate occasions by a number of different divers so the same distance was often measured four or five times. All of the distance measurements were included in the network adjustment along with the 14 depth measurements and the 6 positions provided by the acoustic positioning system. Of the 114 distance measurements a subset of 55 measurements were used to compute the best estimate of position for the whole data set. The whole network fitted together to an accuracy of 17 mm (RMS).[28]

---

[28] 3H Consulting 1997

The targets located around the site were positioned using both the ROVTrak system and tape measures. It was expected that positions would be obtained by measuring from at least four of the control points to the target however in some cases as few as two tape measurements were made. The control point posts were left on the seabed after the SubMap project was over and all the CPs were still in position in 1999 except the CP B: this is likely to have been knocked over when the submarine was moved[29] in 1998.

The seabed around the submarine was flat and featureless but there was some shallow scouring close to the hull itself. It was decided that heights measured on the site would not need to be referenced to a tide datum and that a nominated point on the site itself could be used, in this case control point SC. Relative depths were measured between this point and the other CPs and these depths were incorporated in the network adjustment. A dive computer was used to measure the depths at each CP; the measurements were made on one dive using a dive computer that had been allowed to cool to the ambient sea water temperature. The effects of tide height on depth measurements were corrected by measuring the depth of the tide datum at the beginning and the end of a series of depth measurements where the time of each depth measurement was noted along with the measurement itself. Variations in the reference point depth caused by the change in tide height as the dive progressed could then be recorded and from these the other measurements could be corrected. To minimise error the measurements were made during neap tides and at slack water so the tidal variation during the dive was the smallest. Computed CP depths were less precise at 100 mm as the site is flat and all the depth information comes from dive computer depth measurements.

Hull Position

Survey points on the submarine were positioned using the control network, a point on the bow and one on the stern then two more points on the hull were also positioned, one each fore and aft on the conning tower. These points were used to compute the position and attitude of the submarine as she lay in 1997. The final computed position for the *Resurgam* was:

Geographical co-ordinates: 53° 23.7268 N   003° 33.3308 W   (WGS84)

Heading: 273° T
Roll: 73°   to starboard
Pitch: 2°   Bow up

The designated position from the designation Statutory Instrument (SI 1996/1741) is 53° 23.78 N 003° 33.18 W (WGS84). This is 200 m bearing 062° T from the actual position in 2016. Fortunately the designated area covers a radius of 300 m so the submarine does lie within the designated area. The wreck lies on the seabed in 12 m depth plus tide height which is up to 7 m on spring tides. The tide runs west to east on the flood tide and east to west on the ebb. During spring tides it reaches a maximum of 1.4 knots

---
[29] Bowyer 2000

3 hours before and 2 hours after high water at Liverpool with slack water at high and low tide and during neap tides the maximum current is 0.8 knots. The site appears on Admiralty chart 1978 Great Ormes Head to Liverpool 1:75000 and the nearest harbour is Rhyl, North Wales, 5 nm (9 km) from the site

The seabed on which the *Resurgam* lies consists of a layer of fine silt and sand overlying a gravel and shell substrate with stiff sandy clay beneath. With hand fanning a diver could excavate 200 mm into the seabed with ease. The seabed was flat over the whole survey area within ±0.5 m however there were local variations close to the submarine itself and there was some shallow scouring running west from the submarine. The area around where the *Resurgam* was found is regularly visited by trawlers.

SubMap Wide Area Search

As the mobile sediment on the seabed was known to be only approximately 150 mm deep it was thought that the missing parts of the submarine may lie on or close to the surface rather than being deeply buried in the seabed. A comprehensive search of the seabed was undertaken to locate the missing items using a combination of ROVs and divers. The side scan sonar surveys had identified 23 targets around the submarine. The position quality was poor but the targets could be positioned more accurately relative to the submarine hull as this too appeared on the sonar record. The Slingsby crawler ROV was used as the main search tool for the wider area around the wreck. This gave us the ability to visit all areas within the site and investigate any visible targets at all states of the tide as being a seabed crawler vehicle it was unaffected by currents. The crawler ROV was fitted with a ROVTrak subsea positioning transceiver so its location was known on the site and it could be used to guide the ROV to known target positions. The transceiver was mounted within the ROV roll cage and was connected to the surface system using a separate cable taped to the ROV umbilical that provided power and communications to the surface. The delicate acoustic transducer had to be mounted so that it had a clear line of sight to the four acoustic beacons in frames on the seabed around the submarine; being fixed to the top of the roll cage it was in a very exposed place. So the transducer was mounted on a rubber hydraulic hose fixed to the top of the ROV so that it would bend out of the way if anything hit the transducer during deployment or recovery. The crawler also had a UDI high resolution scanning sonar mounted on the front which could be used to detect any targets on the seabed and provide a range and bearing from the ROV to the target. The seabed was essentially flat over the whole survey area and the sonar was mounted on a stable platform only 1 m above the seafloor so it was well placed to be able to detect targets and any scour pits that had formed in the sediment. The scanning sonar used a high frequency so could be used to detect targets smaller than could be seen using the towed side scan sonar. The crawler ROV also had the advantage that it could locate a target on the seabed and then immediately move closer, homing in on it until the target was close enough to be identified using the on-board cameras. The system was used in conjunction with the acoustic positioning system in an efficient survey of the site extents. The crawler ROV visited all parts of the site and searched for targets from positions all around the submarine, so any partly buried objects not apparent from one direction may be detected from a different direction. All of the targets detected using the sonar were investigated, their positions recorded and images of them were recorded on video. An Aquascan International Ltd. pulse induction metal detector and fluxgate magnetometer were intended to be fitted to the ROV, however these systems were not made available during the SubMap Project.

Diver Search

Divers were used to search areas close to the submarine where it was not possible for the crawler ROV to operate and they were also for the visual and metal detector searches. Any targets found were then positioned using tape measures or the acoustic positioning system. A number of diver-held Aquascan AQ1B and Whites P1000 pulse induction metal detectors were available for use by the search teams. These units were used for location of new targets during searches or re-location of targets that were to be investigated. Both types of detector were used and both types were found to be reliable and effective. The teams of divers doing metal detector searches were provided with markers for tagging any targets that they found; the markers were made from tent pegs with a length of bright orange Netlon netting attached so the Netlon floated clear of the seabed and could easily be seen at a distance. Each diver that located a target was given the task of making tape measurements to it from at least three survey control points so that the target could be positioned and added to the site plan. In addition, the positions of any new targets were obtained by the survey team divers using the APS (Figure 28). Each team was allocated an area to search close to the hull; the areas were usually small, 10 m by 5 m maximum, and were covered more than once by different divers to ensure complete coverage. Working outside the main survey area was more complicated as there were no visual references for the divers to work to so survey areas were marked out with ropes using measurements to the control points as a reference. Targets that were located within the working range of the surface supplied divers were recorded on video using the diver's helmet mounted camera while targets outside this area were recorded using the ROV cameras or diver held video and stills cameras.

Figure 28: Diver searching the seabed with an Aquascan pulse induction metal detector while being tracked by the ROVTrak acoustic positioning system

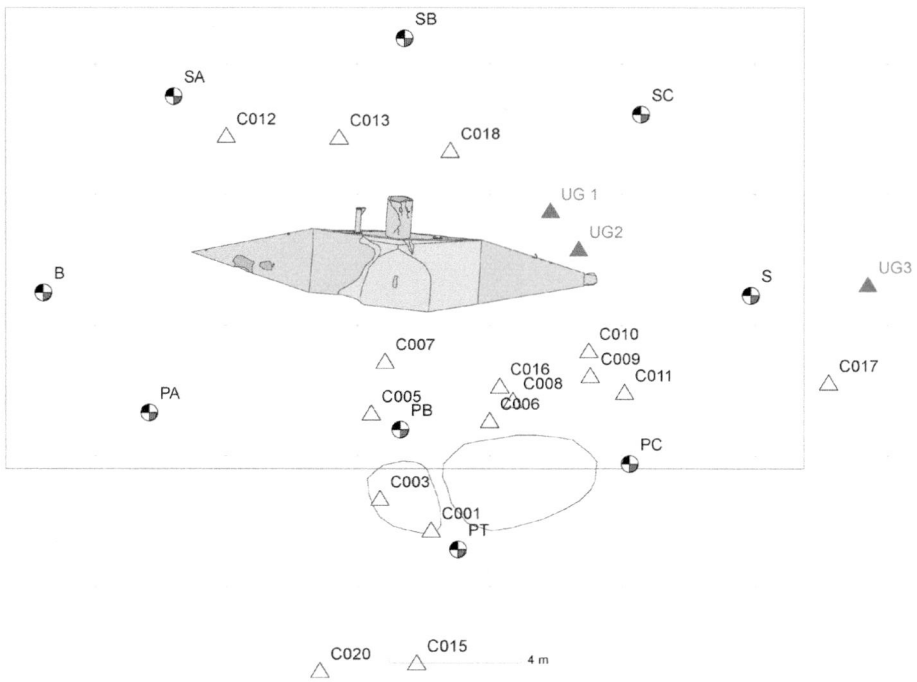

Figure 29: Plan of the site showing target locations on the seabed around the submarine

A total of twenty targets were detected during the search but C002, C004 and C005 were found to be parts of the same object and C019 was the same object as C012. Six objects were excavated and identified and the remainder were not investigated due to lack of time, see Appendix 1 Table 6 and Figure 29.

'Uri Geller' Targets

During the survey we were offered the services of the well-known celebrity Uri Geller to assist in locating the missing parts of the submarine. A copy of the site plan was sent to Mr

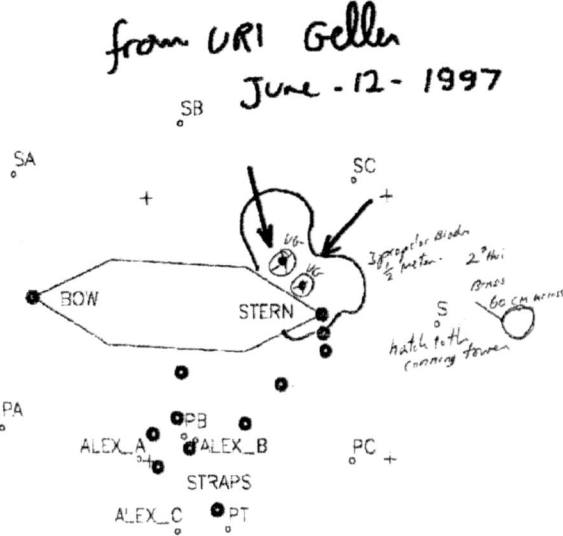

Figure 30: Fax from Geller showing his estimate for the location of the missing objects

Geller and it was returned marked with his estimate of the location of the missing parts, close to the stern on the starboard side (Figure 30). The centres of the areas marked on the Geller plan were set out on the seabed using tape measurements from the control points, see Appendix 1 Table 7. Each point was investigated with a pulse induction metal detector within a radius of 5 m of the centre point and the centres of the identified locations were excavated to a depth of 1 m below seabed level. No targets were found in the areas indicated.

SubMap Hull Recording

The first of the Phase 1 requirements was that the exterior of the hull was recorded in detail and this task was to be undertaken by the Archaeological Diving Unit. The plan stated that the hull external features would be photographed, videoed and drawn at an appropriate scale on a mosaic of sheets of plastic drafting film[30]. Unfortunately this aspect of the project was not completed. A few dive logs from the volunteers were of some use to fill in the missing information as they often contained a sketch, but many were provided with no location information or a series of random measurements between features that were not related to the established survey control; in total only five dive logs from the volunteers provided any useful information. The survey team on

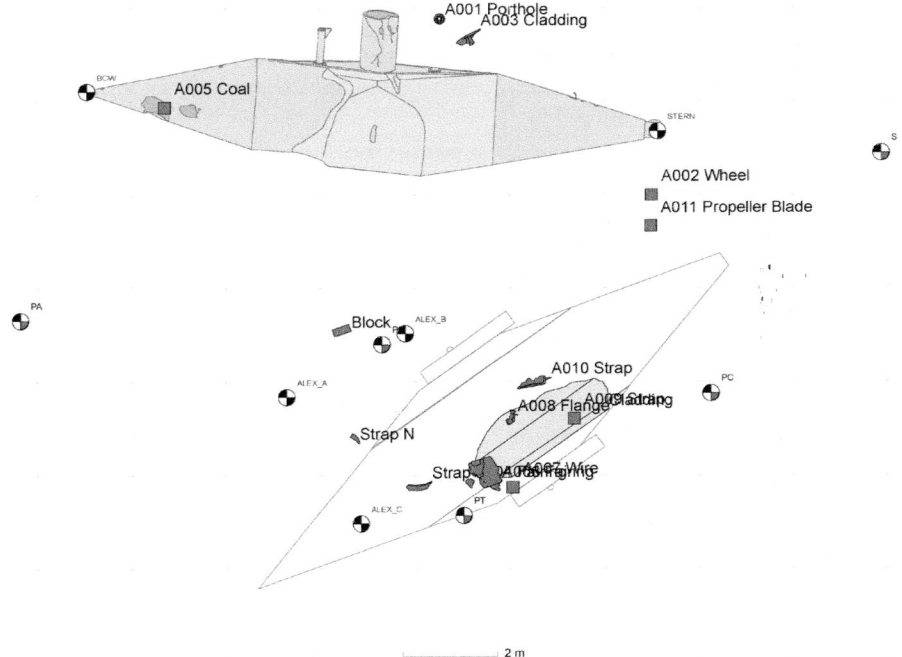

Figure 31: Plan of the site showing the location of artefacts

---

[30] ADU 1997

the support vessel completed a video survey of the hull using the small inspection ROV even though this was not within the given scope of work for this team. The coverage of the hull was systematic and complete and included a 200 mm 3D scale cube where possible and a second video survey was completed on 15th June after the hull had been cleared of marine growth two days earlier. The survey team also completed detailed records of the conning tower, propeller, stern fittings and snorkel.

SubMap Excavation

The SubMap Phase 2 requirements required that any located items be moved to a holding area next to the wreck. This task required the authorisation of limited excavation under license from Cadw.

The main area for investigation centred on a point 6 m to the south of the hull (Figure 31). The two iron straps poking out of the seabed (Strap N by 650 mm, Strap S by 280 mm) had been used to attach the wood cladding to the hull. The straps were firmly fixed in the seabed which suggested that more hull material may lay buried nearby. A trench was opened which initially encompassed the two straps but it was extended in size as buried cladding timbers and finds were uncovered. In 1996 the two straps appeared to be connected together by a metal plate but this was not on the surface in 1997. Six artefacts relating to the submarine were excavated before encountering a substantial portion of timber at a depth of 0.55 m below seabed level (Figure 32). The flat metal plate was found in fragments not deeply buried and lying over pebbles, recorded as fairing (A004 and A006) and other finds included a wire strop fragment (A007), a copper alloy skin fitting from the hull (A008) and a portion of cladding strap (A009). The maximum depth of the trench was 1.03 m with patches of clay at the bottom. The maximum length of timber excavated was 3.1 m from a maximum original length of 4.9 m but not all was uncovered as the unexcavated timber extended both vertically and horizontally.[31]

The angle, shape and length of the timber suggest that this represents a portion of the wooden cladding, probably still attached to the iron straps that held the timber to the hull. The upper edge of the timber exhibited a torn appearance and the upper face retained a strong, black, well-preserved hard surface, suggesting contact with the iron hull for a long period, with some of the iron penetrating into the wood. This feature suggests that the separation of the timber from the iron was secondary to the sinking. The depth and orientation suggests that the submarine may have gone down on her belly, and would have been buried to at least half the height of the pressure hull excluding the conning tower. The depth of burial of the hull and its relation to the survival of the hull timbers is discussed later. Until the excavation trench is enlarged it is impossible to state whether this is lower port side cladding, lower port and lower starboard side cladding, lower starboard cladding or lower and upper starboard cladding (the upper port cladding is present in part). This structure may comprise both lower port cladding and lower starboard cladding and the keel timber may lie beneath it. The wood showed no signs of surface degradation and therefore must have been buried rapidly after sinking and remained buried until the excavation.

---

[31] Hildred 1997

Figure 32: West end of the trench showing the faired timber cladding and iron retaining straps

Raising, Recording and Reburial

In addition to the artefacts excavated within the trench, on the 4th June a number of artefacts found on the seabed were recovered to the surface for recording. All artefacts were lifted, kept in seawater tanks aboard the support vessel, recorded, then reburied within the excavation trench having been first wrapped in polythene and then placed into crates. The trench was stabilised with sandbags and refilled using a fire hose attached to the crawler ROV to jet sand into the hole, a method that proved both swift and effective.

The objects were reburied at: 53° 23.72 N   003° 33.33 W   (WGS84)

The objects are buried 11 m from both the bow and the stern of the submarine in her location in 2016.

3D Models

With the submarine lying on its side and the visibility limited it was initially difficult to understand the layout of the site so a scale model of the submarine was constructed from beer cans as an aid to understanding, see Figure 33. Later, a three-dimensional model of the submarine was created using AutoCAD as shown in Figure 34.

Figure 33: The beer can model of Resurgam

Figure 34: A 3D digital model of Resurgam created in 1997

SubMap Finds

The finds from the site that were recovered, recorded and reburied are listed below.

A001 Porthole Iron and brass porthole 225 mm φ overall with a 75 mm φ glass window and a rubber seal, with the remains of four of the six 20 mm φ bolts or rivets that attached it to the conning tower. Surface find, reburied in the trench. This was found on the seabed beneath the conning tower in an area that had been previously searched using a metal detector, so it is likely that this had been returned to the site by one of the visiting sports divers. 53° 23.7277 N 003° 33.3295 W	
A002 Steering wheel Two fragments of the six-spoke iron hand wheel Surface find, reburied in the trench. 53° 23.7258 N 003° 33.3254 W	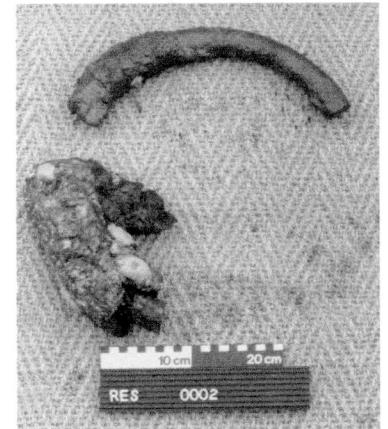
A003 Cladding Timber cladding fragment Surface find, loose, reburied in the trench. 53° 23.7274 N 003° 33.3290 W	

A004 Fairing Small fragment of iron plate from the fairing or cutwater, part of A006. Excavated from 500 mm depth. 53° 23.7224 N 003° 33.3289 W	
A005 Coal A lump of coal, probably from the bunker in the bow cone. Loose, reburied in the trench. 53° 23.7262 N 003° 33.3346 W	
A006 Fairing Large fragment of iron plate from the fairing. Excavated from 500 mm depth. 53° 23.7229 N 003° 33.3284 W	

A007 Wire Strop

Fragment of wire strop.

Excavated.

53° 23.7224 N 003° 33.3280 W

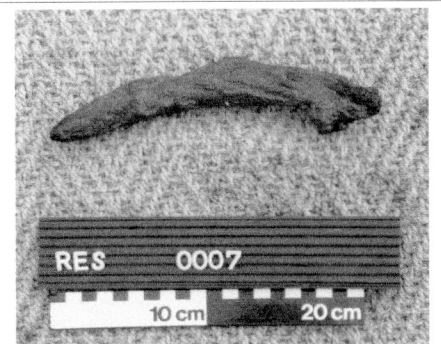

A008 Skin Fitting from the outside of the cladding

Copper alloy, iron, wood, concreted.

Excavated from the trench.

Based on its location in the trench, this fitting may have been the inlet for cold water for the condenser which was mounted low down in the hull on the starboard side, just in front of the engine. A pipe attached to the fitting would have passed though the wood cladding to allow in sea water.

53° 23.7234 N 003° 33.3282 W

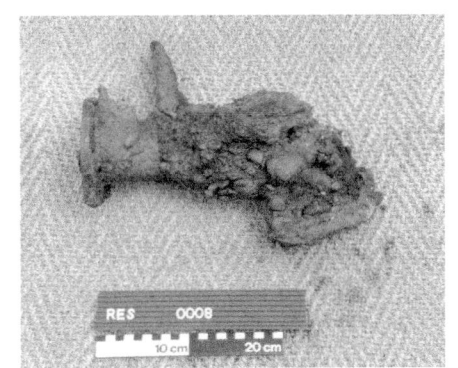

A009 Strap

Part of a metal strap 80 mm wide used to attach the wood cladding. The narrow width suggests that it is part of the broken strap that was attached around the forward edge of the cladding.

Excavated.

53° 23.7232 N 003° 33.3268 W

A010 Strap L section end fragment of a strap for retaining the wood cladding, including the remains of the bolt that pulled the two ends of the strap together. The narrow width suggests that it is part of the broken strap that was attached around the forward edge of the cladding. Heavily concreted, excavated. 53° 23.7234 N 003° 33.3279 W	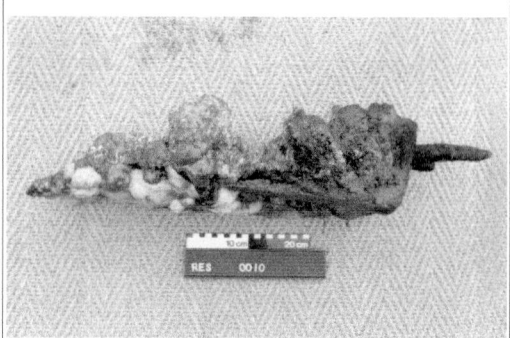
A011 Unidentified / Propeller blade Metal detector contact found 2 m south of the stern of the submarine. 53° 23.7254 N 003° 33.3254 W, Point C010	
C001 Strap N, C003 Strap S Straps for attaching wood cladding, most likely to be from the forward end of the submarine as this section of cladding was missing from the hull. 53° 23.7230 N 003° 33.3310 W, Point C001, C003	

C005 Block Iron block covered in concretion, 370 mm x 160 mm and at least 140 mm high, partially exposed, use unknown. 53° 23.7241 N 003° 33.3314 W, Point C005	
Cladding Large section of timber cladding at the bottom of the trench, maximum length excavated was 3.1 m x 1.1 m wide. 53° 23.7234 N 003° 33.3279 W	

SubMap Corrosion Study

A further Phase 1 requirement was the measurement of the corrosion potential of the iron hull and the attachment of sacrificial anodes. This work was done by Dr David Gregory who at the time was a project leader at the Danish National Museum's Centre for Maritime Archaeology. The work is described in detail in the paper *In situ corrosion studies on the submarine Resurgam, A preliminary assessment of her state of preservation*[32] and the text below is taken from it.

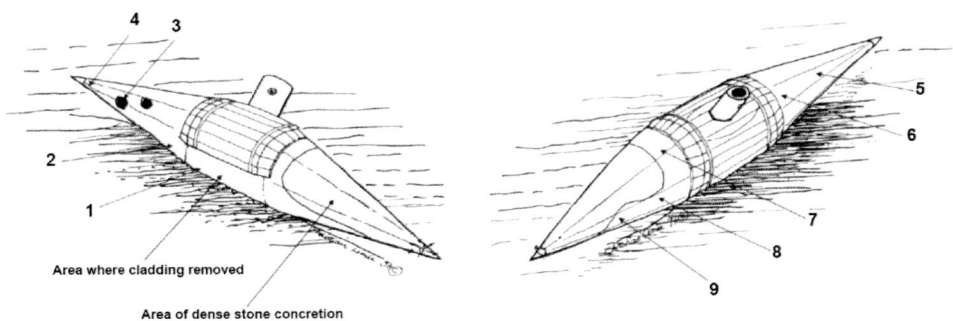

Figure 35: Sketch of the site showing features referred to in the text (adapted from Gregory)

---

[32] Gregory 2000

Nine points were sampled; all the points lower down on the hull had thicknesses of between 1-3 mm but the points along the upper deck had thicker corrosion with point 5 at 12 mm, point 6 at 9 mm and point 7 at 15 mm (Figure 35).

The results of this preliminary corrosion survey indicate that *Resurgam* is actively corroding, although the mechanism is such that the corrosion products are most likely to be of a protective nature. The present corrosion rate is hard to quantify based on established means as the nature of the wrought iron means that the complete concretion profile was not retained over the entire hull. Certainly, moving the submarine from her original resting place will have accelerated the corrosion rate, especially in the areas which were previously buried or covered with wooden cladding. However, based on the areas where the concretion profile was retained it would appear that areas exposed to sea water for the past 116 years have been corroding at approximately 0.10 mm per year. This combined with the knowledge of the corrosion rate of freshly exposed wrought iron enable a prediction of a present 'worst case' corrosion rate of between 0.1 and 0.2 mm per year.

In addition to monitoring the corrosion potential and surface pH, two series of anodes were attached to the *Resurgam* to lower the corrosion potential and hence the corrosion rate. Two anode arrays, each consisting of five 2 kg zinc anodes were bolted onto a section of a car axle which was connected to a G clamp with heavy-duty insulated six core copper cable. One array was placed at the large hole on the port side towards the bow near measurement Point 3 while the other was attached to the conning tower. The corrosion potential was measured at these locations before and one day after the anodes were attached and the immediate effect was to shift the potential by -0.04V. This is not sufficient for complete protection but the results were encouraging; considering the large surface area of the submarine compared with that of the anodes, it will take time to re-polarize the massive electrode. However, the anticipated lifespan of the anode arrays was calculated to be between 25 to 35 days and the anodes had been exhausted between one and three months after their attachment.

Considering the surface area of the hull (90 m^2), if it were to be stabilized in situ, or relocated to a wet dock and stabilized, it has been calculated using the aforementioned guidelines that 125 kg of zinc would be required per year to provide complete cathodic protection.

SubMap Marine Biology Survey

The first phase of the SubMap project called for a biological survey of the wreck and its environs then the recording and removal of the marine life on the hull prior to detailed hull recording. The site was surveyed by the Joint Nature Conservation Committee (JNCC) Marine Nature Conservation Review (MNCR) team based at the Centre for Environment, Fisheries and Aquaculture Science (CEFAS) Laboratory in Conwy on the 29 May 1997. This coincided with the start of the SubMap Project coordinated by the Archaeological Diving Unit.[33] The aim of the survey was to identify and give approximate abundances

---

[33] Holt R. 1997

for all conspicuous species present on the wreck and surrounding seabed prior to any disturbance from other divers taking part in the SubMap programme. MNCR recording techniques were used and results recorded on MNCR recording forms. The abundances given in this report and on the recording forms relate to the SACFOR (Superabundant, Abundant, Common, Frequent, Occasional, Rare) abundance scales. Separate records were made of the wreck of the submarine and of the surrounding seabed. The species found were as follows, in taxonomic order:

Species found on the wreck		
Species	**Abundance**	**Common name/comments**
Tubularia indivisa	Occasional	Oaten-pipe hydroid, characteristic of strong tidal streams
Diphasia rosacea	Frequent	A common hydroid, forms much of the fine 'fuzz' over the wreckage
Obelia sp.	Frequent	A common hydroid
Metridium senile	Superabundant	Plumose anemone- the dominant anemone over much of the wreckage. Common in strong tides. Both orange and white forms are common. This species readily divides to reproduce asexually
Sagartia elegans	Common	Sagartia anemone - smaller anemone with an orange and brown striped pattern. Also common in area with strong tides
Polydora sp.	Superabundant	A very small worm (polychaete) which forms thin mud-tubes protruding from the surface of the substratum. In this case a large number of the worms had bored into the wood covering parts of the wreck. In other situations this worm is capable of boring into limestone issuing an acid secretion to aid the process
Balanus crenatus	Superabundant	A common barnacle species (crustacean) which occurs on many tide-swept hard surfaces. It had colonized much of the wreck's surface
Amphipod indet.	Occasional	Amphipods (a general term which includes sand-hoppers) are sometimes regarded as fouling organisms as they produce large aggregations of 'parchment' tubes over the surface of stone and wooden parts of the wreck. Probably Jassa sp.

Hyas araneus	Rare	'Sea toad' spider crab. Only a few found on the wreck
Hyas coarctatuseus	Rare	Spider crab. Only few found on the wreck
Cancer pagurus	Occasional	Edible crab. A few found on the wreck and in small cavities
Necora puber	Occasional	Velvet swimming crab. A few found over wreck
Archidoris pseudoargus	Occasional	'Sea lemon' nudibranch, a large sea slug. A few were found over the wreck
Aeolidia papillosa	Frequent	A medium sized sea slug which predates on sea anemones
Hiatella arctica	Occasional	A small bivalve mollusc which bores into soft rock, clay and wood. In this case it had bored into the wooden cladding of the submarine
Asterias rubens	Common	Common starfish – found commonly in most habitats in this region
Trisopterus luscus	Common	Bib - a fish common on wreck sites
Trisopterus minutus	Common	Poor cod - a fish common on wreck sites
Taurulus bubalis	Common	Sea scorpion - a small spiny fish common on hard substrata in the region
Labrus bergylta	Occasional	Ballan wrasse - common in the region
Pholis gunnellus	Frequent	Butterfish-a small eel-like fish often common on hard surfaces
Callionymus lyra	Occasional	Common dragonet - small bottom dwelling fish common in the region

Species found on the seabed

Corymorpha nutans	Rare	A solitary hydroid which lives on the surface of the sand
Tubularia indivisa	Rare	Se above
Hydrallmania falcata	Frequent	A hydroid characteristic of tide-swept and sand scoured conditions
Sertularia argentea	Occasional	A hydroid characteristic of tide swept and sand scoured conditions
Sertularia cupressina	Occasional	A hydroid characteristic of tide swept and sand scoured conditions
Alcyonium digitatum	Occasional	Dead men's fingers- on cobbles and pebbles, more common on larger rock and bedrock in the region

Cerianthus lloydii	Common	Burrowing anemone - a common species in mixed sediment, reacts quickly if disturbed
Urticina felina	Rare	Dahlia anemone - attaches to hard substrata or pebbles buried in sand; common throughout the area
Metridium senile	Occasional	See Above
Sagartia elegans	Rare	See above
Chaetopterus variopedatus	Frequent	A large polychaete worm which forms a parchment tube either buried in sediment or attached to hard substrata
Lanice conchilega	Occasional	Sand mason worm - common in sandy sediment
Pomatoceros triqueter	Rare	Keel worm - common elsewhere on pebbles
Balanus crenatus	Frequent	See above, although on stone in the sediment
Hyas araneus	Occasional	See above
Hyas coarctatus	Occasional	See above
Cancer pagurus	Rare	See above
Necora puber	Rare	See above
Buccinum undatum	Rare	Common whelk- scavenger on sandy habitats
Doto sp.	Occasional	A small nudibranch which lives on hydroids
Alcyonidium diaphanum	Rare	A sea mat bryozoan - this one forms brown jelly-like stalks growing up from the substratum
Electra pilosa	Frequent	A fine lace-like bryozoan which covers many different substrata
Asterias rubens	Common	See above
Opiura albida	Rare	A brittle star often found on sediment habitats
Trisopterus minutus	Common	See above
Taurulus bubalis	Occasional	See above
Callionymus lyra	Occasional	See above
Pleuronectes platessa	Frequent	Plaice - common flatfish on sandy sea beds

Discussion

The fauna present on and around the wreck of the *Resurgam* is very typical of the tide-swept conditions. The large number of *Metridium senile* and *Sagartia elegans* found here are characteristic of the many wrecks and rocky substrata in the area. Sand stirred up during heavy seas has a scouring effect when swept against the wreck by the tides and this is reflected in some of the scour-tolerant species such as the hydroids *Sertularia argentea* and *Sertularia cupressina* and the bryozoan *Alycyonidium diaphanum*. Another common species, although small and relatively inconspicuous, is the barnacle *Balanuscrenatus* which encrusts many of the available hard surfaces of the wreck. Fish are obviously attracted to the wreck which offers refuge and a source of food and those present are typical of the region. There are a number of animals which are slowly degrading the submarine's wooden cladding. In particular, the small polychaete worm *Polydora* and the boring bivalve mollusc *Hiatellaarctica* dig into soft wood and will probably eventually degrade its structure completely. The other species recorded are typical of rock and sediment habitats in this part of Wales. Species-richness is not particularly high and none of the species recorded are regarded as being particularly rare or unique to the habitat surveyed.

Later Site History

After SubMap

After the 1997 SubMap project, local licensees Richard Bufton and Mike Bowyer visited *Resurgam* to monitor the condition of the wreck and re-attach sacrificial anodes when necessary. To further plans for the management of the site an interim Resurgam Committee was set up by the Royal Naval Submarine Museum in 1996 which was followed by the independent Resurgam Trust in 1998.

Sometime after the SubMap survey, probably in spring or summer 1998, the *Resurgam* submarine was moved. In 1999 the ADU conducted diving operations on the site and confirmed that the wreck had shifted position, stating that the wreck had rotated on its axis and now lay with a list to starboard of about 10°. They reported seeing an unknown metal structure on the port side of the wreck which they later interpreted as possibly being part of a lifting cradle.[34] In June 1999 the site was visited by Mike Bowyer and a police diving team but they found no conclusive evidence that the submarine had been interfered with, other than that it had moved.[35]

In 2000 they revised the identification of a metal structure on the port side of the wreck from being the remains of a lifting frame to an actual structural element of the wreck itself.[36] This was likely to be the remains of one of the four iron straps that were used to hold the timber cladding on to the hull. When the timber was knocked off the hull one of the straps may have remained in place and this could have been interpreted as part of a cradle in poor visibility. In 2004, site licensee Mike Bowyer recorded the inside of the hull using a camera mounted on a pole. In July 2006 one of the portholes removed from the wreck was donated anonymously to the Receiver of Wreck which was then given to the Royal Navy Submarine Museum for curation.[37]

2007 Wessex Archaeology Site Assessment

In 2006 Wessex Archaeology was commissioned by Cadw to undertake a Designated Site Assessment of the *Resurgam* submarine.[38] The work was undertaken as part of the Contract for archaeological Services in Relation to the Protection of Wrecks Act (1973). At the time the report on this work was the most complete summary of the state of the submarine. The observations about the state of the hull were made nine years after SubMap and after the submarine had been moved for a second time in 1998. The fieldwork involved confirming the shifted position of the submarine, with the positioning being done using a Sonardyne Prospector APS which was the successor to the ROVTrak system trialled during SubMap.

---

[34] ADU 1999a
[35] Bowyer 2000
[36] ADU 2000a
[37] Wessex Archaeology 2007
[38] Wessex Archaeology 2007

In the new position the hull was lying across the tidal currents and this survey noted that the hull was affecting the seabed sediments, with a shallow scour around the wreck extending approximately 0.3 m under the submarine in most places but up to 0.4 m on the starboard side. The report confirmed that the wood cladding present in 1997 had disappeared from the hull but the hull itself was largely covered in plumose anemones so many of the detail features were hidden.

Observations from the report include:

- On the top of the bow cone is a hole 60 mm ϕ which is suggested to be a deadlight or free flood
- Just behind the hole is a small glass deadlight 60 mm ϕ on the upper centreline for illumination of the stokehold and bilge pump
- A hole in the bow cone is reported as being 0.8 m x 0.65 m, with delicate edges showing recent corrosion
- An 'internal dividing section' is noted at the wider, aft end of the bow cone
- Anode attached to the lower edge of the bow cone hole with a G clamp
- Inside the hole the sand/silt 50 mm towards the bow and 200 mm against the 'bulkhead' aft
- The hull is actively corroding with noted areas of fresh corrosion
- Air intake 0.76 m forward of the conning tower, which agrees with the existing site plan
- Intake is cylindrical 0.8 m high, with an 'amorphous concretion' thought to be the counterbalance for the automatic shutdown valve
- The conning tower has an anode attached, but the shape of the top has changed since 1997
- Identified port side hydroplane shaft bent up at a an angle of 90°
- Stub of fairing max. 100 mm high where it attaches to the pressure hull aft of the conning tower
- Two eroded anodes are attached to the fairing stub
- Hole in the hull in the stern immediately forward of the propeller for the vertical rudder shaft
- Propeller had an anode attached using a G clamp
- Three scaffold poles which were used as survey control points were noted and positioned but the report omits to mention which ones they were

After 2007

In 2007 a team from Trafford Sub-Aqua Club placed new sacrificial anodes on the submarine to help slow electrolytic corrosion.[39] In 2009 the site plan and digital document archive was published using Site Recorder 4 to make the data available so that a report on the submarine could be written.[40] In 2012 a group of divers from Chester BSAC put more sacrificial anodes on the hull.[41]

---
[39] Manchester Evening News 2007
[40] Holt 2009
[41] BBC 2012

Site Formation

We can use information from the archaeological investigations to estimate what happened to the submarine itself between its loss in 1880 and the present day. The evidence on the seabed suggests that changes happened in three separate phases.

Position A – 1880 to 1993

Evidence suggests that after sinking the *Resurgam* submarine became buried or partially buried in the seabed, lying on an even keel at a point 7 m to the south of the 1997 surveyed position (Figure 36).

Centre	53° 23.723 N	003° 33.328 W	
Heading	235° T	±10°	
Roll	0°	±10°	(estimated)
Pitch	0°	±5°	(estimated)

The evidence for this was found in the bottom of the trench excavated in 1997 where hull cladding timbers were found buried at a depth of 550 mm below seabed level. The attitude of the timbers in the trench provides a clue about the original alignment of the hull which gives us an estimate for the vessel's heading, roll and pitch. Engineer Price's account suggests that the boat foundered under tow and at high water, with

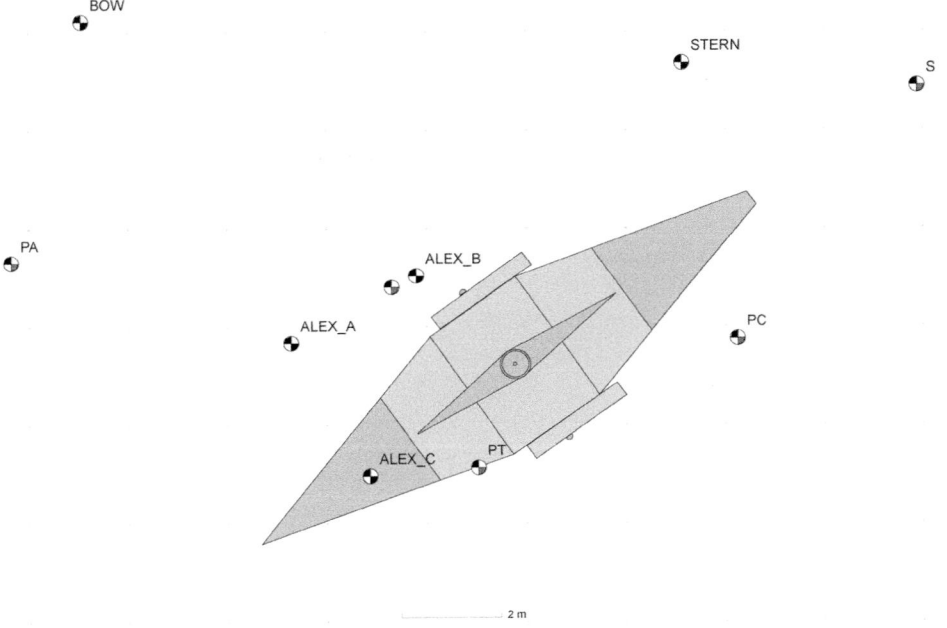

Figure 36: Site Plan for Position A with the hull upright and buried in the seabed

a 7.7 m tide height, the depth was 20 m. Even so there would have been only a short time between the 12 m long boat sinking and her hull hitting the bottom. Even if the submarine flooded quickly the impact may have been quite gentle so it is unlikely that she would have lost sufficient buoyancy and gained enough momentum in that short time for her to plough deeply into the seabed.

It is likely that the submarine was lighter at the bow than the stern because she had burned some coal which was stored right up forward, a place where the loss of mass would have a significant effect on her trim. If she were trimmed bow up any water entering the hull would migrate quickly to the stern, further raising her bow and making the problem worse. In this position she would sink stern first and land on her propeller, breaking off the blades in the process, which may be one reason why they are missing. Once full of water the submarine would have lost all buoyancy so it is unlikely she would have drifted far in the tidal current and if this is the correct sequence of events the impact point should be close to where the buried timbers were found.

The submarine sitting on the bottom would have formed a significant obstruction to tidal flow. Scouring of the seabed under the hull of the submarine would form a pit in which the hull would eventually partially or completely bury itself. A fragment of fairing from the 'deck' of the submarine was found in the excavation trench so it is possible that the fragment survived because it fell in to the scour pit that had formed under the hull and eventually became buried. The actual depth to which the hull was buried is not known but there are a number of clues, some of which are contradictory. From the date of sinking to when she was found, the submarine could have been on the surface, half buried, buried up to the deck, completely buried or a selection of those options at different times in her life.

There is a good case for the hull being completely buried, or buried up to the lower edge of the conning tower (Figure 37).

- If the hull was completely buried then it explains why it was not detected during the geophysical survey in September 1992 or during a number of previous geophysical searches, as all that was noted was a trawl scar
- If the hull was only half buried then the 1990's sonar equipment used in the early searches would easily have detected it, which suggests that the hull was buried deeper because it was not detected
- If the hull was completely buried apart from the conning tower then the same sonar should have detected the 2 ft wide tower on a flat seabed, but perhaps not if its shadow was masked by the much larger trawl scar
- The area is frequently visited by trawlers so if the hull had been above seabed level then it is quite likely that she would have snagged a trawl net much sooner, which again suggests that she was buried deeper
- Wood will rapidly erode and decay in UK seawater unless it is buried. Timber cladding was still attached to the hull in 1997 so this must have been buried and thus protected

- The timber in the trench showed no signs of surface degradation, and therefore must have been buried rapidly after sinking and remained buried until the excavation
- There is an area of concretion toward the stem which had stones up to 100 mm in diameter incorporated into its matrix and these stones are only found deep under the soft sediment found in the area
- There is a difference in the concretion found on the lower part of the hull and the concretion found on the upper deck and conning tower. Gregory noted that the concretion on the deck was much thicker at between 9 and 15 mm whereas the hull concretion was only 1-3 mm thick.[42] The concretion on the conning tower was noted to be 10 mm thick where it was still attached (Figure 45). This difference is consistent with the hull being buried up to the conning tower where the tower and the upper deck are subject to oxygenated water and the rest of the hull in an anoxic environment as it is buried in the seabed

At first glance the evidence from the excavation trench suggests a shallower burial. The two straps N and S appear to be the broken remains of the strap that was once around the forward end of the cladding as this strap is missing from the hull on the seabed. The maximum depth of the trench was 1.03 m with the cladding timber still continuing both vertically and horizontally, and the maximum length of timber excavated was 3.1 m of a maximum timber length of 4.9 m. But the top of the cladding that would have touched the iron hull was only 550 mm below seabed level; in this condition the hull would only be buried to half the height of the pressure hull (Figure 37). However, it is possible that whatever caused the hull to have been extracted from the seabed may have pulled the cladding upwards from an original, deeper position and it finally separated from the iron hull at the depth of 550 mm where it was found.

One hypothesis put forward was that the submarine sank under tow, dived towards the seabed and buried itself completely into the seabed like an anchor. This is extremely unlikely to have happened as the submarine only had 20 m depth in which to accelerate downwards. The seabed

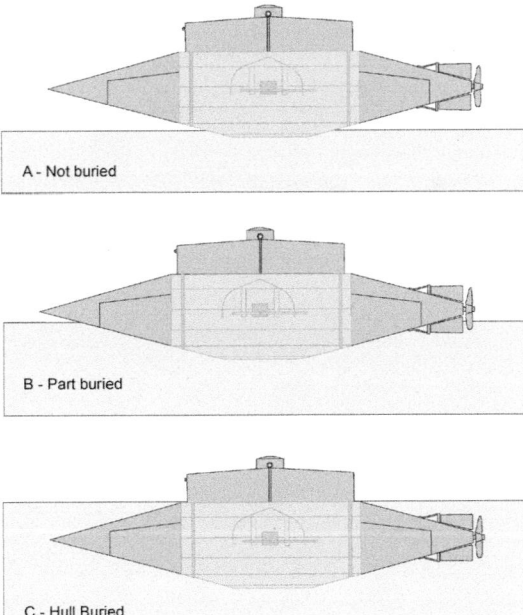

Figure 37: Three options for burial of the hull in the seabed

---
[42] Gregory 2000

in the area is quite hard under a thin layer of soft sediment so the forces involved would be severe enough to damage the bow. The diver surveys and photographs show that the bow is undamaged and is in good condition so it is not likely that the Resurgam sank and was buried while being towed.

Position B – 1993 to 1998

At some point the submarine appeared above the seabed, moved 7 m to the north and rolled hard over on her starboard side at an angle of 73° (Figure 38).

Centre	53° 23.727 N	003° 33.331 W
Heading	274° T	
Roll	73°	to starboard
Pitch	2°	bow up

If the submarine was sufficiently buried in the seabed for it to be hidden from side scan sonar surveys and the many trawlers that operate in the area, why did it suddenly appear and snag the nets from Dennis Hunt's boat in 1995? The submarine weighs 30 tons so considerable force would have to be used to pull it from the seabed, drag it 7 m and roll it on to its side. It has been suggested that this was the work of a beam trawler but this seems unlikely if the hull was buried, and if it was hit while upright hard enough to move the hull then it is likely that the conning tower would have been ripped off. A possible clue about why this happened is the two large holes in the bow cone where damage to the hull consists of a ~1 m square hole with another further aft approximately

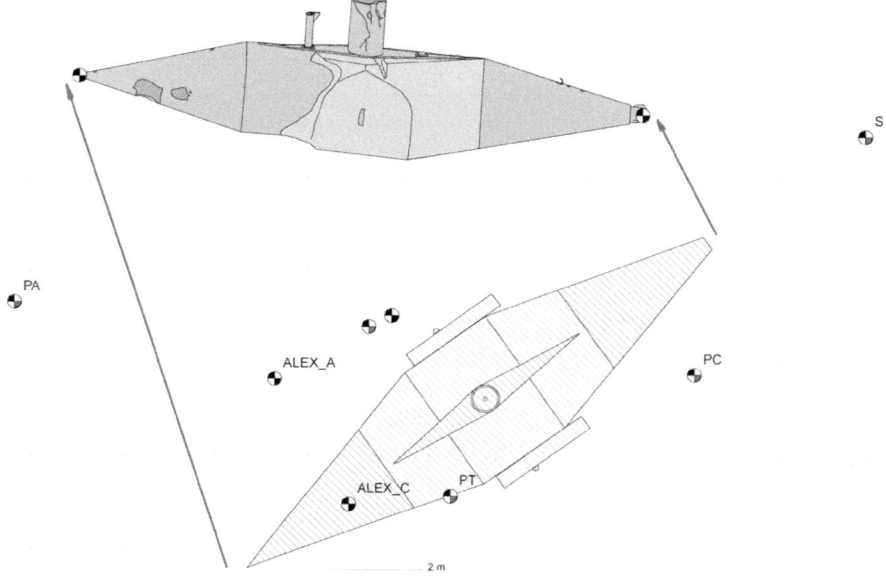

Figure 38: Site Plan for Position B showing movement of the hull from A to B

0.25 m square. An area of hull plating had been pushed inwards around the larger of the two holes and the smaller was where the bilge pump had been attached to the inside of the hull; the plating at this point is now bent inwards with the pump still attached. The most plausible theory is that the damage was caused by a modern stockless ship's anchor. A ship may have deployed its anchor on the seabed and dragged the anchor into the buried submarine where the anchor flukes dug in to the hull. Later when the anchor was recovered the submarine may have been pulled bodily from the seabed and dragged six metres before rolling over and releasing the anchor from the iron plating. The dent in the conning tower may have been caused by the anchor striking the top of the tower as it swung free of the hull.

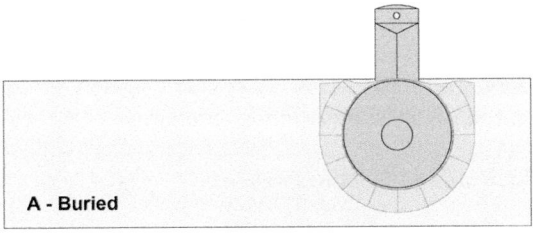

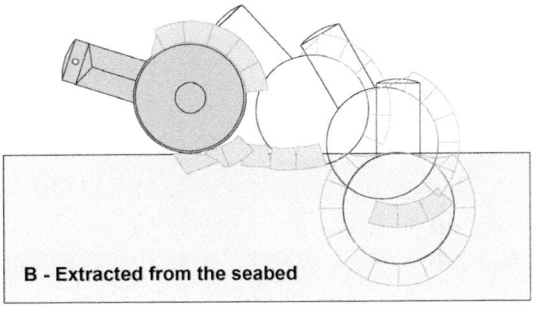

Taking into consideration all the evidence there are a number of possible explanations for the sinking and disappearance of the submarine. Although the evidence is not overwhelming, the following train of events is favoured by the authors:

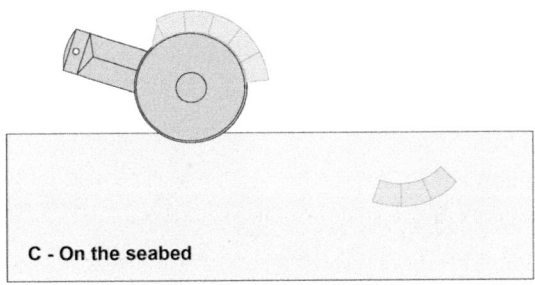

Figure 39: Proposed site formation sequence

- The submarine was buried in the seabed up to the base of the conning tower
- A large vessel hooked its anchor into the bow of the submarine
- When the anchor was recovered the submarine was pulled out of the seabed, leaving some cladding timbers and straps behind.

This process is shown in Figure 39. The iron hull and wood cladding are initially buried up to the conning tower (A). The hull is pulled from the sediment (B); the lowest cladding timbers remain attached until the straps break. The lower timbers are then left behind and remain buried along with the broken straps (Strap N, Strap S). The port side timbers remain attached to the hull. The starboard timbers are ripped from the hull as it is dragged 6 m sideways and the broken pieces are left to wash away in the tide. The site is left with the hull lying on its side, port side timbers in-situ and lower timbers buried in the seabed (C).

When the submarine was found in 1995 the seabed around it was flat and sandy with very little scour and only a small accretion of sediment under the hull. A scour pit has formed around the hull since that time which suggests that the submarine had not been on the seabed for very long when it was first seen.

Position C – 1998 to Present

In August 1998, Mike Bowyer's team dived on the site in poor visibility and discovered that the submarine had moved. At some unknown date that year the submarine had again shifted, this time 4.8 m to the west and she had rolled more upright (Figure 40).

Centre	53° 23.726 N	003° 33.335 W
Heading	210° T	
Roll	10° - 14°	to starboard[43]
Pitch	Unknown	

When the submarine was moved for the second time what remained of the timber cladding was knocked from the hull and the conning tower top was crushed together. Again, there were a number of reasons put forward at the time.

- Bowyer suggested that this was caused by severe storms in January and February 1998, somehow associated with air being trapped in the submarine[44]

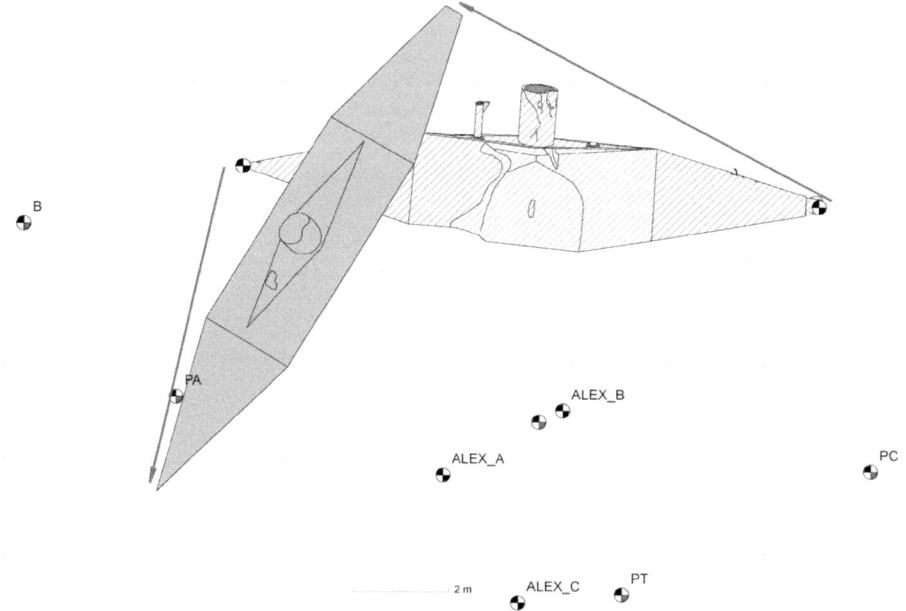

Figure 40: Site Plan for Position C showing current position and attitude of the hull

---
[43] ADU, Bowyer SRC-2000-1
[44] Bowyer 1999

- Beam trawlers were suggested as the cause. This is very unlikely as all of the survey control points installed around the hull in 1997 were still in place except one[45]
- The movement may have been caused by a failed salvage attempt

The survey done by the ADU in 1999 recorded strapping around the hull and the remains of a lifting cradle, but this was done in very poor visibility so reliable identification was impossible.

The submarine is now lying at almost 90° to its 1997 alignment, across the prevailing currents and on top of control point PA which was bent over and is lying flat on the seabed. Although the visibility was less than 0.5 m a search of the area failed to locate any of the timbers lying on the seabed in the vicinity as reported by the previous visitors. These timbers had presumably been washed away in the strong tidal currents that sweep the area. There is a previously unrecorded dent in the hull on the portside amidships.[46]

One idea that had been suggested was that the submarine had been snagged in one of the four mooring ropes from the dive support vessel *Terschelling* when they were recovered at the end of the SubMap fieldwork in 1997, and that the large ship had pulled the submarine over as she left. However, this could not happen as the mooring lines were made of buoyant rope; the rope would float once it was released from the anchor

Figure 41: Large diameter floating mooring rope attaching the ship to an anchor buoy in the distance

---

[45] Bowyer 2000
[46] ADU 99/07

buoy it was shackled to before being reeled in to the vessel (Figure 41). With all ropes reeled in the anchors were recovered in turn; these too could not have snagged the submarine as the closest was 267 m away from the wreck.

Now that the submarine is lying across the alternating tidal current it appears to be reburying itself in a scour pit forming under the hull; at spring tides the current can reach 3 knots. Silty sand is also beginning to accumulate around the hull so the pointed ends at bow and stem are now close to the seabed.

Resurgam Today

The condition assessment below describes each part of the submarine in detail, what we know about it and any factors to consider during subsequent fieldwork.

The Hull

The pressure hull of the submarine was in remarkably good condition in 1997 apart from the two large holes in the bow plating. In essence the hull seen by the divers was same hull described in the design documents and in the plans shown in the article in the Engineer journal. When first seen the hull was covered in anemones with a few patches of fresh corrosion visible on the plating. This often happens on flat plates on iron ships where the weight of the marine life growing on a plate provides sufficient force to remove the upper corroded surface and expose fresh metal underneath. The hull was scraped clean of marine life on 13th June 1997 during the SubMap project to allow detailed recording, with one example shown in Figure 42. This task was not done carefully so this also removed some of the corroded metal surface. In 2006 Wessex noted a similar situation where the hull was covered in anemones but there were new areas of fresh corrosion.

Hull plating thickness measurements were not made on the hull in 1997. The original thickness of the hull is not accurately known; the Cochran's quote from 7th April 1879 was for 3/4 in (19 mm), 5/8 in (15.9 mm) and 1/2 in (12.7 mm) plating and this was assumed to be 3/4 in for the main hull cylinder with perhaps 5/8 in for bow and stern cones. However this may not be what was actually used. Gregory provides a 'worst case' corrosion rate of between 0.1 and 0.2 mm per year. By 2016 the submarine had been on the seabed for 136 years which gives a total loss of between 13.6 mm and 27.2 mm in total. Based on these calculations the 19 mm thick main hull cylinder could only have 5.4 mm thickness of metal remaining or nothing remaining if the larger loss value is used. The submarine is still on the seabed and still largely intact so perhaps the calculated rate of corrosion is an over-estimate. As a comparison, the rate of loss calculated from ultrasonic hull thickness measurements on the steel hulled submarine HMS/M *A7*

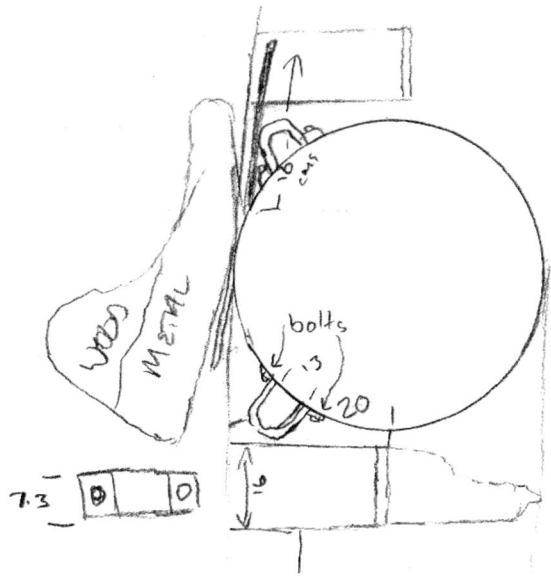

Figure 42: Plan sketch of the conning tower base

built in 1903 was 0.058 mm per year.[47] Note that in the 20 years since the submarine was first found an estimated 16% more plating thickness has corroded away. On riveted iron shipwrecks it is common to find that the rivets holding the plates together have corroded faster than the plates. No information is available to suggest this is the case with the *Resurgam* but it is a subject that needs investigation. If the rivets do corrode faster than the plates then the hull is likely to collapse at the seams, particularly the longitudinal lap joints used to hold the main cylinder plates together. It is not known if the *Resurgam* was built with an internal frame as the available documents differ in their conclusions and they may not reflect what happened in practice. This is another subject that requires further investigation as it is a crucial factor in estimating how long the hull will survive before collapsing in on itself.

In 1997 two large holes were noted in the bow cone on the port side. The holes were approximately rectangular with rounded corners with the 1 m square forward hole larger than the 0.25 m square hole aft (Figures 43 & 44). The plating at the edges of the holes appeared to have been pushed inwards as if the holes had been made by something striking the hull and piercing the plates. The larger hole was sealed off with steel plates in June 1996 to stop divers entering the hull but by July the plates had been removed by sports divers. By 2006 just one hole was reported in the bow, 0.8 m x 0.65 m, with delicate edges showing recent corrosion and an anode had been attached to the lower edge of the bow cone hole with a G clamp.[48]

On the top of the bow cone right forward is a hole 60 mm ϕ which Wessex suggested was a deadlight or free flooding hole. On the *Engineer* plan the hole is not shown but what it goes in to is shown as a hollow casting. The Wessex photograph of the hole shows a conger eel living in it so the space inside must be large enough to accommodate one.[49] It makes no sense to have a deadlight in this position so it may be to allow the casting to flood, in which case there should be a matching drain hole underneath. Just behind the hole is a small glass deadlight 60 mm ϕ on the upper centreline for illumination of the stokehold and bilge pump[50] and this was also noted during the survey in 1997.

When the submarine was first inspected in 1996, the two deadlights in the stern cone that were mounted over the engine instruments had recently been cleaned of marine fouling, it was thought prior to their removal by a sports diver.[51] A sketch on a dive log by Garrett from 11 June shows a hole on the upper centreline of the hull forward of the propeller then another 550 mm forward of that. One of the two holes was where the vertical rudder shaft was fitted, probably the forward of the two as 1.56 m further forward was the remains of the rudder bracket which was bolted to the main hull. The remains of the bracket were bent upwards and forwards and it is not known if the bracket still remains on the hull as it was not reported by Wessex. The purpose of the hole aft by the propeller is not known as it is not shown on the plans, but it may have the same purpose as the similar hole in the bow cone casting.

---

[47] Holt 2015, p76
[48] Wessex 2007
[49] Wessex 2007
[50] Wessex 2007
[51] Newell 1996

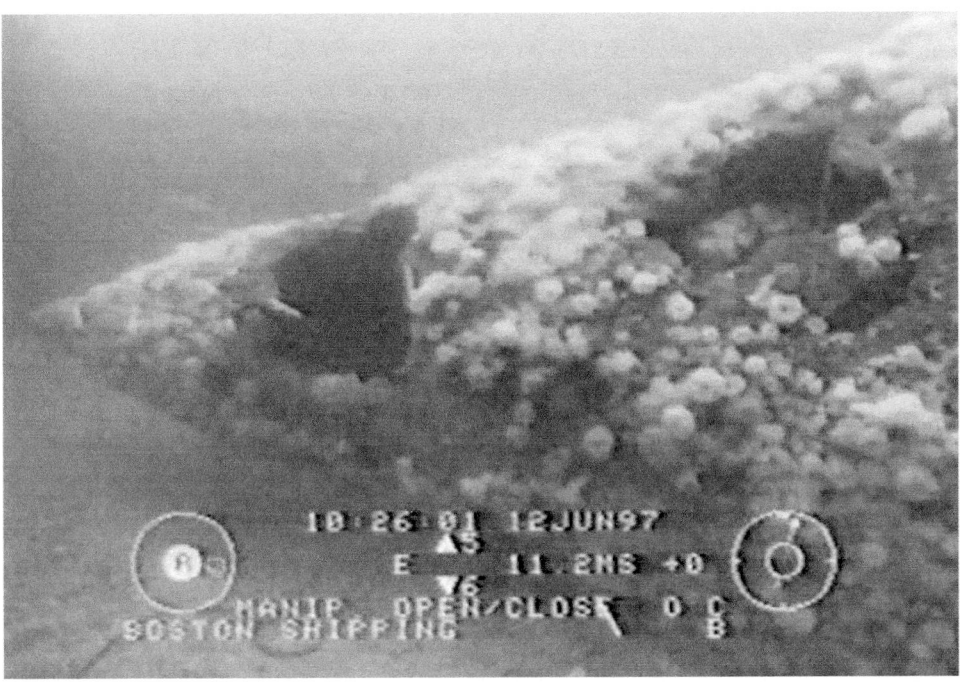

Figure 43: Video image of the two holes in the bow cone

Figure 44: The top of the forward hole in the bow cone showing plating pushed inwards

Conning Tower

The top of the 3 ft tall conning tower was approximately circular in section when it was first seen in 1996 but there was a large V shaped dent on the aft port quarter which had cracked and torn the plating along the folds. The shape of the dent suggests the impact was a direct hit from something heavy that then bounced off rather than the direct blow that would have occurred from a beam trawl. The damage also had to be made by something not too heavy or fast moving otherwise it would have ripped the conning tower from the hull.

Access to the conning tower was sealed off in June 1996 to stop divers entering the hull but by July that year the barrier had been removed by sports divers. In addition, two portholes that had been in place in the conning tower had been forcibly removed and a cast iron steering wheel inside the conning tower had been shattered, with parts of it dropped on the seabed nearby.

The record of the conning tower from 1997 shows that the concretion on the tower plating varied from 10 mm thick over the undamaged area to little or no concretion on the damaged area (Figure 45). This suggests that the concretion had formed uniformly over the plating before whatever impact that caused the dent knocked some off, so the dent in the conning tower may be a recent occurrence. After the submarine moved in 1998 it was noticed that the top of the conning tower had been crushed together which

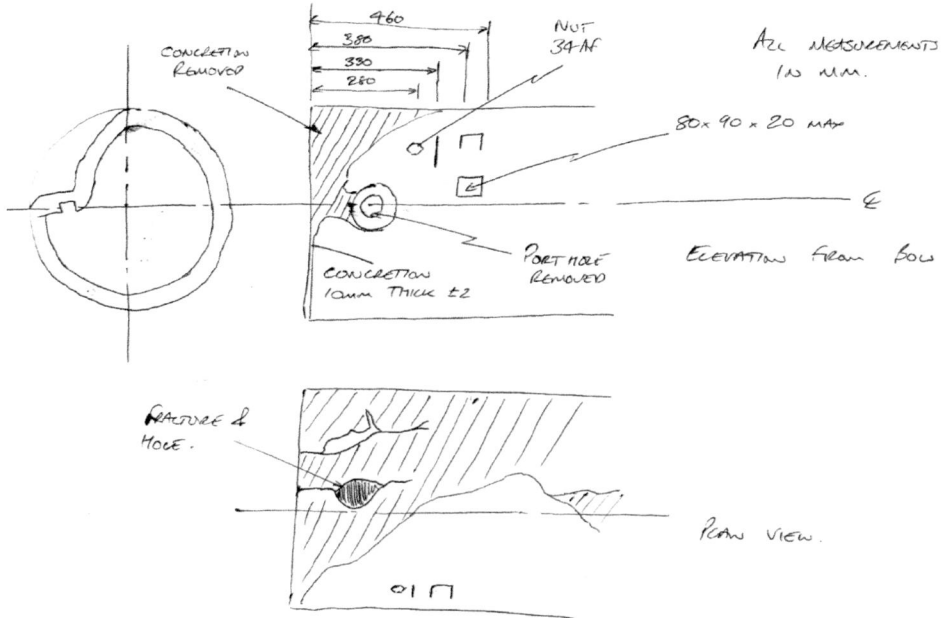

Figure 45: Sketch of the top of the conning tower from 1997

narrowed the entrance to the hull. Wessex noted the alteration to the shape of the entrance and also noted the accelerated corrosion in the damaged area.[52]

Four notches in the inner rim of the tower can be seen in the photographs although only one is shown in the sketch. These notches may have been associated with the mechanism used to close the hatch. The sketch of the tower also shows a 34 mm AF nut on the forward side of the tower; the nut is just off centre and under the porthole. Below this is a square feature 80 mm x 90 mm and 20 mm high. The four portholes fitted at cardinal points around the conning tower are all missing. When the submarine was first seen it is reported that two of the portholes were still in place but were subsequently removed in July 1996 by sports divers.[53] The aft and port side portholes would have been pushed out of position when the impact occurred that caused the dent. The inward folds in the conning tower plate run through two of the porthole holes (Figure 46). This is curious as we have three of the four portholes, two presumably removed by divers from the undamaged locations but one of the portholes must have been from the aft or port, which begs the question about where the third was found. If the damage to the conning tower happened when the submarine was upright then the displaced portholes would have fallen inside the hull. If the damage happened later when the submarine was lying in the 1997 position then it is possible for the displaced portholes to fall into the conning

Figure 46: Photograph of Resurgam in 1997 from behind the conning tower looking forward. The scale cube in the large dent is 200 mm each side

---

[52] Wessex 2007
[53] Dean 2007

tower where they could be retrieved. One of the portholes was found by Keith Hurley in 1996 lying inside the conning tower, it was recovered then given to Bill Garrett: '*It was then that I found one of the sub's portholes, lying inside the conning tower, having popped its rivets, and I brought it back up.*' [54] Garrett's porthole is kept in sodium carbonate solution in a low light area with the solution changed every six months. It has visible cracking of the cast iron flange which was present when Garrett was given it, but cracks are now wider. One porthole was found on the seabed during SubMap, under the conning tower in an area that had been previously searched using a metal detector, so it is likely that this had been returned to the site by one of the visiting sports divers. This porthole was given the finds number RES_A001, photographed, traced and then reburied in the excavation trench. A third porthole was handed to the Receiver of Wreck who passed it on to the RN Submarine Museum for conservation and curation but the fourth porthole is still missing.

The conning tower hatch is missing - this would be an important object to locate as where it was found may provide clues as to how the submarine was lost. The hatch opened horizontally towards the bow so the pivot point would have been on the leading edge of the upper conning tower rim. Had the hatch been ripped off as described by Price it is likely that this would have damaged the rim of the conning tower at the attachment point; however no damage in this area was recorded.

Fairing

The fairing around the conning tower was missing in 1997 apart from fragmentary remains of the bottom edge of the plating where it attached to the top of the pressure hull. A section of the thin plating used for the fairing (A006) was found in the bottom of the excavation trench in 1997. The iron plating was thinner than the pressure hull so would have corroded and fallen off sooner, ending up in the scour pit under the hull where it became buried. Bowers suggests the fairing may have been removed[55] but this seems not to be the case. In 2006 Wessex reported that the lower edge of the fairing a maximum 100 mm high was still visible where it attaches to the pressure hull aft of the conning tower and two eroded anodes were attached to the fairing stub.[56] The air intake or snorkel was used to allow air into the boat when the main hatch was shut and the submarine was running on the surface. The snorkel is a 0.8 m long, 160 mm diameter tube mounted vertically through the pressure hull with a self-sealing copper alloy valve mounted on the top. In 1997 the tube and valve were in-situ but the float for the valve was missing and the same tube and valve were reported by Wessex in 2006. Aft of the conning tower was the exhaust for the engine; in June 1996 the exhaust pipe was missing but a 20 mm diameter copper alloy rod which was part of the mechanism for closing the exhaust vent was still in place, but by July that year the rod had been sawn off.

---

[54] Gorton 1996a
[55] Bowers, p118
[56] Wessex 2007

Timber Cladding

A section of the timber cladding that originally surrounded the cylindrical part of the hull was still in place in 1997, reaching round to within 1.3 m of the seabed on the port side. The cladding was originally formed from 14 truncated wedge sections of timber and this construction method could be seen in 1997 by the way the remaining timbers had separated from the missing ones in clean breaks. The timber still on the hull was the eroded remains of five of the full wedge sections running from the port side deck down towards the keel, forming a strip approximately 1.8 m long around the hull. The lowest section was 3.94 m long with the timbers getting progressively shorter towards the conning tower. The cladding was attached using four iron straps, each in two semicircular pieces with flanges at the ends where two bolts would be used to fasten them together: the two at the ends of the fairing were 80 mm wide and the two either side of the conning tower were 160 mm wide. It is possible that the individual timbers were also joined together with additional pins but no evidence for this has been found so far. In 1997 two of the straps which would have held the cladding to the hull were visible above seabed level so the area around them was excavated. The two straps visible on the surface were found to be two ends of a single curved strap that held the timber to the hull at the bow end of the cladding. Sections of cladding were also found at the bottom of the excavation trench, again with flat, straight sides where the individual timbers had separated. The upper edge exhibited a torn appearance and the upper face retained a strong, black, well preserved hard surface, suggesting a contact with iron for a long period, with some of the iron penetrating into the wood. This suggests that the separation of this cladding from the hull was secondary to the sinking. It is thought that the buried timbers may comprise both lower port cladding and lower starboard cladding, and that the keel area may lie beneath it. The wood showed no signs of surface degradation therefore must have been buried rapidly after sinking and remained buried until excavation in 1997.

Rudder and Hydroplanes

Any remains of the two vertical rudders have not been seen on the submarine, nor any remains of the vertical shaft they were attached to. The rudders would have been made of thin iron plate so would have corroded away quite soon and the shaft may have corroded quickly if it had been attached to copper alloy bearings. The holes through the stern where the shaft passed through were noted in 1997 and again by Wessex in 2007. The bracket attached to the hull forward of the rudder shaft that supported the shaft itself was drawn by Garrett in 1997 but was not noted in the 2007 Wessex report.

The *Resurgam* was fitted with a three-bladed propeller when it sank. The diver's sketch from 1997 shows the three remaining stumps where the propeller blades broke off. In 2006 it was noted that the propeller boss had an anode attached to it using a G clamp.[57] Artefact 97A011 was found 2 m to the south of the stern of the submarine and is thought to be a fragment of propeller blade.

---

[57] Wessex 2007

No remains of the two hydroplanes have been seen on the site but visible on the port side are the remains of the single shaft through the hull they were attached to. In 1997 the shaft passed through the remains of the wood cladding and a short section was visible, bent upwards towards the conning tower. In 2007 this was noted as being bent up at an angle of 90°.[58] It is not known whether the starboard side hydroplane is still attached to the hull as the hull was lying on that side during the 1997 survey.

Hull Interior

The inside of the submarine has not been investigated as gaining entry would be extremely difficult and space on the inside is very limited. It is rumoured that a number of divers have climbed inside the stokehold through the hole in the bow cone but it is thought that they could progress no further as access to the stern is blocked by the large boiler and accumulated sediment. The interior of the hull was not officially investigated during SubMap other than to take sediment depth measurements; inside the bow cone there was 50 mm of sediment towards the bow and 200 mm close to the boiler. A sketch by Garrett from 10th June shows sediment built up on the starboard side of the hull, filling the space between the starboard side and the boiler to a maximum depth of approximately 0.5 m. An 'internal dividing section' was noted by Wessex at the aft end of the bow cone but this could only be the forward end of the furnace and boiler. Divers did attempt to gain access to the submarine prior to 1997 via the conning tower where they succeeded in breaking the steering wheel in the process. It is not known if anyone was successful in their attempts or if any portable objects or easily removed items from the engine are now missing. It would be a shame if the inside had been disturbed as what was found, or not found, inside the hull may tell us more about events surrounding the loss of the submarine.

Site

In 1997 a shallow scour and associated ridge had formed in the seabed under the starboard side of the hull.[59] Since the hull moved in 1998 and now lies across the tidal currents it is causing a new scour in the seabed with a shallow pit forming to the east, deeper pits at each end of the hull and a low bank on the starboard, western side.[60]

The state of the excavation trench was not reported by Wessex in 2007 but the seabed in the area appears flat and featureless in the Bibby Hydromap multibeam image (Figure 47). The aluminium posts used as survey control points have been noted on subsequent visits after 1997 but in 1999, after the submarine had moved for a second time, the ADU noted that the hull was now lying on top of survey point PA which was bent over flat on the seabed. Three poles were noted and positioned in 2006 by Wessex but the report omits to mention which ones they were. Bowyer reported that all the survey posts were still in place except one, CP B which lay to the west of the hull[61], but did not mention the state of survey point PA.

---

[58] Wessex 2007
[59] Hildred 1997
[60] Osiris 2011
[61] Bowyer 2000

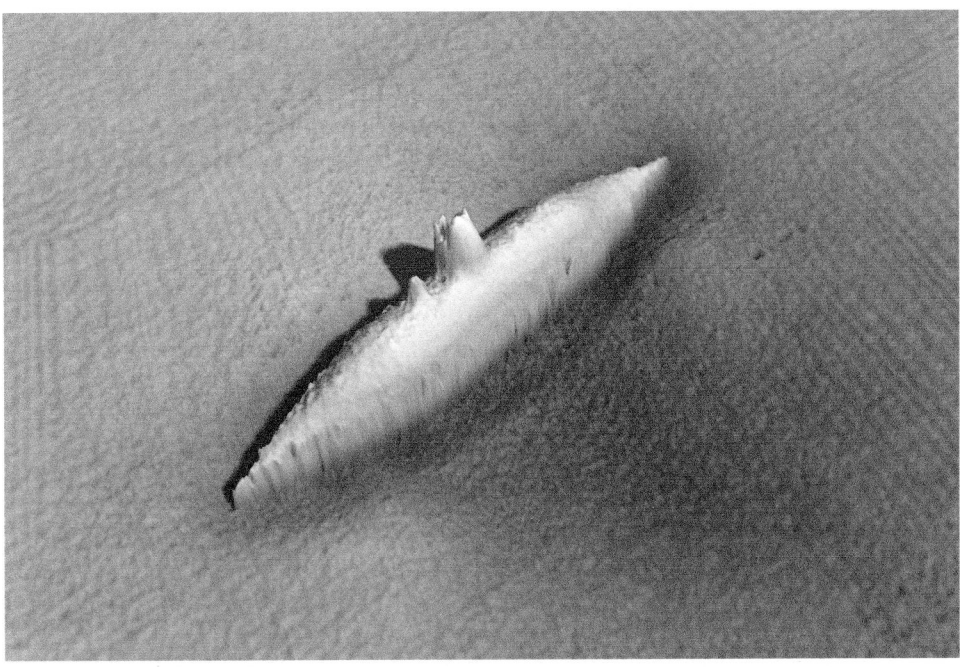

Figure 47: Multibeam sonar image of Resurgam from 2011 (Bibby Hydromap Ltd.)

A Reanalysis of the Loss of *Resurgam*

Documentary sources say that *Resurgam* set out from the harbour at Rhyl at 10pm on 24th February, 1880, in the company of the steam yacht *Elphin* as escort. At some point in the voyage the engine of the *Elphin* started giving trouble so the 3 man crew on *Resurgam* transferred to the escort ship to help with repairs. At this point *Resurgam* was taken in tow by *Elphin*, but once the *Elphin* was underway again the crew could not be transferred back to the submarine due to rough seas. At 10am the next morning the tow rope parted and *Resurgam* disappeared beneath the waves. This sequence of events has raised a number of questions which warrant further investigation.

Why did Garrett report the submarine lost off Great Ormes Head, 20km away from where she sank?

Great Ormes Head is the nearest notable land feature to the sinking position, lying some 20km to the west, but the nearest town was Rhyl only 9km away (Figure 48) so it is surprising that he did not report the loss to be 'off Rhyl'. At an estimated speed of 3 knots, or 5.6 km/h, *Resurgam* would have been past Great Ormes Head after just five hours at sea. The two vessels departed at 10pm and the submarine sank at 10am the next morning, so it is curious that after 12 hours at sea the submarine ended up on the seabed so close to the harbour he had departed from. One suggestion was that the submarine drifted across the seabed after she sank - if the submarine slowly took on water until it disappeared off Great Ormes Head it could possibly have drifted with the tide if it had remained nearly neutrally buoyant. But the submarine sank at 10am, just 30 minutes before high tide, so for the next six hours the tide would be dropping and the current would be heading west rather than east back towards Rhyl. The current was in the wrong direction to take it back towards Rhyl for the time when the boat would have been most buoyant. Garrett may have deliberately given a plausible but incorrect location to stop others salvaging the submarine before he could make an attempt. It is odd that the *Elphin's* crew did not attempt to mark the place where the submarine sank so that it could be more easily relocated and salvaged later on, or perhaps they did and this was never recorded. Bowers[62] also noted that

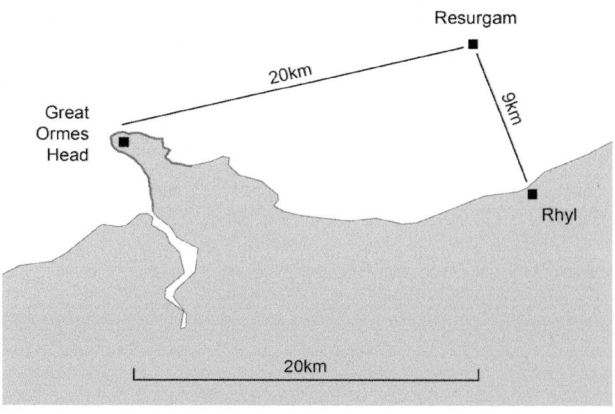

Figure 48: Plan showing the wreck location relative to Great Ormes Head and Rhyl

---
[62] Bowers, p121

no record has been found of Garrett informing the coastguard of the loss of the submarine, which if it had been awash rather than sunk would have been a significant hazard to navigation. The day after the loss Garrett travelled back to Liverpool by train to get assistance to search for the submarine, but nothing further was done as the weather was still poor. What is surprising is that an attempt to recover the submarine was not tried once the weather had cleared. Perhaps this was done but Garratt managed to keep the story both from the newspapers and the other source for this story, the engineer George Price.

Did the *Elphin* ram the *Resurgam*, dent the conning tower and sink her?

It is possible that the tow vessel hit the submarine accidentally just before she sank but it is unlikely that she was rammed deliberately; the submarine was well built so the ramming vessel may have come off worse in the attempt. In any case it would not be necessary to ram the submarine as simply leaving the hatch open in a rough sea would flood and sink the ship in a very short time. But the clues provided by the portholes and the iron concretion suggest that the large dent in the conning tower happened sometime after the submarine sank.

Was the conning tower hatch taken off deliberately?

Bowers[63] attributes the sinking to the conning tower hatch having been '*shattered*', quoting engineer Price in the story he told to the press many years later. But this raises a question about the ability of the sea to 'shatter' the hatch while leaving the rest of the conning tower undamaged. The hatch has never been found; this may be because it still lies on the seabed some distance from the submarine or because it has been recovered by a souvenir-hunting sports diver. If the hatch 'shattered' then it may no longer be in one piece. This still leaves the question why the top of the conning tower shows no sign of the hatch being forcibly removed. When the finder Keith Hurley was interviewed by Diver magazine in 1996, he recalled that:

> '*Apart from the sharp dent in the conning tower, I was very surprised to see that her main hatch had been removed - not ripped off, but clearly taken off*'.[64]

No sign of damage to the conning tower at the attachment point was seen when the tower was recorded in detail by the author in 1997. It is worth noting that Garrett's 1878 Patent for the prototype *Egg* submarine includes the statement that:

> '*I arrange the roof of the conning tower so that it is easily taken off if anything happens to the boat, so that the occupants can rise to the surface, being aided by life belts if desired.*'

---

[63] Bowers, p120
[64] Gorton 1996a

Being a significant safety feature it is possible that this idea was carried over to the hatch fitted to the top of the conning tower on *Resurgam* and perhaps this special feature was used in earnest. It is possible that the hatch was removed deliberately if the intent was to scuttle the submarine as this would be a simple means of ensuring that the hull would flood quickly. Garrett did not expect anyone would ever see the submarine again so any evidence of its removal would never come to light. But a further detailed investigation into the state of the top of the conning tower may provide more clues about what really happened to the hatch as would another sonar search for the hatch on the seabed near the submarine using modern high resolution methods.

Why were all of the crew taken off the submarine when they knew the hatch could not be shut from the outside?

Murphy[65] claims inability to adequately secure the conning tower hatch from the outside was the reason the submarine flooded and sank. However, correspondence from the builders Cochran & Co. indicate that as part of the conning tower they fitted '*one manhole with screw inside and out*', which suggests that the hatch could be closed from the outside (Figure 14). If this were the case then it should have been impossible for the vessel to take on water due to the sea breaking over her - the main hatch on the submarine is all that stands between the crew and oblivion so it is inconceivable that the mechanism used to close it was anything but secure. There were three people on board at that time they left the submarine to repair *Elphin*, so even if it were not possible to secure the hatch from the outside it is reasonable to think that one could have been left behind to lock the hatch after the others had left. Only one person was needed to fix the engine so two could have stayed, even if it meant they had to be taken in tow. Another small but illuminating detail is mentioned by Murphy; when called to help on board the escort '*the crew all took their kit to the yacht with them*', an action that may be considered odd when they were only off to repair their escort rather than abandoning ship. Even the ship's tiny pennant was saved from the submarine; Captain Jackson brought it from the boat when he left and presented it to his sister who still had it 40 years later.[66] We may never know what really happened but a careful examination of what remains inside the submarine may show if the crew were ever intending to return.

How did the submarine sink?

The cause of the sinking is attributed to flooding through the conning tower. The reserve buoyancy of the submarine was very small so it would not require much water to flood the hull for it to sink, even though she would ride a little higher after three men (~250kg) had been removed and some of the coal had been burnt. If the flood water came in slowly then the submarine would gradually get lower in the water until it became neutrally buoyant, eventually becoming heavy enough to gently sink to the bottom. Very little water would be required for this to happen and certainly not a significant mass would be required in comparison with a submarine displacing 30 tons.

---

[65] Murphy, p73
[66] Murphy, p73

If the water leaked in slowly then the small mass required to sink the boat would not have put sufficient additional strain on the tow rope to cause it to break. If the water came in quickly then the submarine would have sunk like a stone to the seabed which would increase the drag sufficiently to break the tow rope or tear the towing fitting from the submarine. But again, one wonders why the catastrophic flooding happened some time after the crew left the boat; if the hatch could not be sealed well enough to stop a major ingress of water then the submarine should have sunk almost straight away as so little seawater was required to sink it.

It is likely that the *Resurgam* towed very badly because of her shape and because the tow point on her hull was high up on the leading edge of the fairing. With the tow point high up, the towing force would constantly be pulling the bow downwards which would tend to make the submarine dive. If the submarine did not sit directly behind the *Elphin* when being towed then the high tow point would also tend to pull the submarine sideways so that she rolled over on her beam ends, further complicating any unruly behaviour under tow. Experience by the author of an autonomous submarine of a similar size to *Resurgam* found that under tow it would snake to port and starboard, making extreme excursions of its own free will, and the only solution to the problem was to steer the submarine by remote control as it was being towed along. The tow rope would have been put under severe shock loads when trying to tow a capering submarine in a rough sea, which may explain why the rope eventually broke.

Fact and fiction

As often happens with a shipwreck story, we are left with as many questions as we have real answers. One option to consider, however awkward and uncomfortable, is that the tale of her loss as told by Price is a complete fabrication. Garrett said very little about the loss other than the provably untrue statement about her having been taken from the harbour and Price's version contains many glaring errors which cast doubt over its veracity. The crucial question to answer is why Garrett would need to make up a story? But if we look at the situation he found himself in we can perhaps hazard a guess at his motivation. As well as being a talented young engineer, Garrett was a salesman and he had a company to promote. On 17 January 1880, while the *Resurgam* was being modified in Rhyl and just a month before the submarine disappeared, the Graphic magazine reported that '*this boat, the inventor tells us, is in every way a success, and will easily perform what has been expected of her*'. Like many salesmen in this more modern age, he may have just been saying what the customers wanted to hear. Privately he may have realised that *Resurgam* would not ever work; she had no ballast tanks to sink her and not enough engine horsepower to drive herself underwater, so she was never going to function in the way he had promised the Royal Navy and his other prospective clients. The few days stay in Rhyl part way through the journey to Portsmouth extended into two months; partly this would be caused by the usual poor winter weather but perhaps some of the delay was caused by Garrett deliberately postponing the inevitable. This raises questions about why they ended up in Rhyl at all; surely it would be better to test the submarine at sea then return to Birkenhead where any problems could be dealt with by Cochran & Co. who built her? Perhaps Garrett chose to move to Rhyl to be away from the prying eyes of the local press who were at the time keen to report each trial and test of the submarine. Leaving Birkenhead would be a wise strategy if Garrett had doubts that the submarine would be a success and although Rhyl had minimal port facilities it did have a nearby foundry that could make new components for the boat. Once the *Resurgam* left Rhyl to continue her journey she could never return without serious damage to Garrett's professional credibility, so the submarine would either have to get to Portsmouth or sink in the attempt. Either way, he had bet everything on the success of the submarine.

Perhaps Garrett thought he could manoeuvre his way out of this financial disaster. Garrett tried to get the Admiralty to cover his losses a short time after the submarine disappeared which they understandably refused to do.[67] Did Garrett really think that he had an arrangement with the Admiralty where he had been making a submarine for them and thus they were liable for the loss, or were these simply the actions of a man attempting to recoup his losses by any means possible? Garrett was still selling shares in the submarine company six months after the only asset had been lost[68] and he was telling reporters that he had '*already made several voyages in the boat constructed upon his plans*'.[69] The arms dealer Thorsten Nordenfelt may have been forefront in his mind when Garrett was deciding what to do; Murphy states that Nordenfelt and Garrett met in 1879[70] and hints that Nordenfelt may have provided some financial backing for the development of *Resurgam*. Crucially, Garrett knew that Nordenfelt had the funds that he needed to build a bigger and better submarine, one with a big enough propulsion system and space for ballast tanks. The result of collaboration with Nordenfelt in 1884 was the development of the *Nordenfelt 1*; at 56 tonnes and 19.5 m long she was nearly twice as heavy as *Resurgam*, yet the new boat had a 100 hp steam engine which was 16 times the size of the engine *Resurgam* had been fitted with. So the design of Garrett's very next submarine highlights the inadequate size of the little 6 hp engine in *Resurgam*. More importantly, this also shows what the ingenious Garrett could do when provided with better resources. Perhaps *Resurgam* was a submarine design that had been limited by available funds and who knows what Garrett could have developed if he had access to the same extensive resources available to Monturiol, his well-funded Spanish rival in submarine design?

Back in Rhyl in the winter of 1880 the situation was bleak; the submarine did not work well enough, they were late for the appointment with the Royal Navy and *Resurgam* was the company's only asset other than Garrett's own reputation as a submarine engineer. With everything at stake desperate measures may have been required. If the submarine was somehow 'lost' at sea, Garratt's failure to appear in Portsmouth with the submarine would be seen as an act of God rather than the result of his own limitations. This would leave the 28 year old Garrett's reputation intact, the only useful asset the company possessed, and he would be free to go on to develop more submarines with the Navy, Nordenfelt or anyone else. Murphy notes the strange tales about the submarine that

---
[67] Dash 1990, p66
[68] Murphy, p75
[69] Manchester Courier 1880b
[70] Murphy, p55

appeared after her loss, suggestions that she had disappeared from her moorings in Rhyl while the crew were at dinner, perhaps stolen by Russian spies. These tales circulated despite the eyewitness accounts of her leaving Rhyl escorted by the yacht *Elphin* and the tales were never corrected by those present at the time. It is understandable that Garrett wished to keep the details about the loss of the submarine out of the press but tellingly it seems he even managed to keep it from his own family. Some years later when Garrett's brother wrote about the events surrounding the loss of the submarine he said that the boat had been lost from her mooring in Rhyl.[71] This tale was still being repeated by the Rhyl Journal in November 1925 in an article about the 'ship that never returned', saying that:

> 'It was at Rhyl the voyage ended. No one can say what happened to the Resurgam, for she was missing one evening when the crew came back from enjoying a meal ashore.'

The alternative version of the story in which the submarine sank under tow was told by engineer George Price and published in the Liverpool Echo just one month after the Rhyl Journal article. It is odd that Price chose to tell his story at that time; it was 45 years after the events happened and by now he must have been an old man. Perhaps he was spurred on by the newspaper article from November, but what motivated him to say anything at all? By now Garrett and Captain Jackson were deceased; they were the two main witnesses to the day's events and they had taken the true story with them. By 1925 many of the other witnesses in *Elphin's* crew may have passed on as well. With few left to argue with what was said, Price could tell whatever story he liked so long as it was plausible, at least more plausible than the submarine simply drifting away. In his version the tiny submarine does leave Rhyl as the newspapers at the time reported, but the events at sea as Price tells them do not match with where the *Resurgam* was finally found so it seems that story is flawed too. Unfortunately none of *Elphin's* crew ever came forward with a different version that could give us more clues about what really happened.

To biographer Bill Scanlan-Murphy, the suggestion that Garrett had scuttled *Resurgam* was 'mildly hilarious'[72], but there are just too many holes in the story and clues on the seabed for us not to consider this as a possibility. The explorer Syd Wignall suggested that Garrett scuttled the submarine[73] as far back as 1975 prior to the first seabed search he helped organise. The drastic step of scuttling *Resurgam* to save a valuable engineering reputation may have been a gamble worth taking. Any sale of a Garrett submarine still relied on having a fully-functional boat because no government would pay for a failed attempt. Perhaps the last-ditch effort to save the situation was to get rid of the evidence on the seabed where they thought no-one would ever find it, and then say it was elsewhere in case they went looking. With reputation still intact Garrett could find more funding to develop bigger and better submarines, and this turns out to be the next chapter in the story of the brilliant, if rather eccentric, George William Littler Garrett.

---

[71] Bowers, p121
[72] Murphy, p74
[73] UCNW 1981

The End?

The development of the *Resurgam* submarine is a fine example of the can-do attitude of Victorian engineers, people who would literally design submarines on the back of an envelope and stake their own lives on the reliability of their designs. Garrett was one of those many men of the cloth of that period who had time on their hands and an interest in more Earth-bound pursuits; some would be naturalists, some would be geologists, while others like Garrett became engineers.

Resurgam is one of the world's first practical submarines and is the oldest surviving powered submarine (Figure 49). The claim that Monturiol built a functioning steam-powered submarine before Garrett is debatable; although better designed and very successful when man-powered, the *Ictineo II* never propelled herself underwater and was hazardous to the crew after only 20 minutes closed up. This train of thought leads to the complex problem of what the word 'working' really means when discussing early submarines. Calculations suggest that *Resurgam* was under-powered and that she could only ever bob under the surface briefly when fully loaded. The addition of the timber cladding hints at a severe buoyancy problem with the original design, a problem cured by the wooden jacket but probably at the expense of her ability to dive. *Resurgam* may have propelled herself underwater only briefly but she was probably the first to do so, yet she was not viable as designed and would not have impressed the Admiralty inspectors she was heading to see when she was lost. *Ictineo II* and *Resurgam* could not have been used for the purpose for which they were designed, so perhaps neither of

Figure 49: Resurgam lying nearly upright on the seabed in 2013 (Justin Owen)

them deserves the accolade for the first steam powered submarine and it should go to some other, later design?

Garrett did have some notable successes to his name, in particular his later Nordenfelt submarines which were the first to be commissioned into any navy. Garrett can be credited for the design of the snorkel as a means of providing air to an engine in a submarine running awash. Unfortunately he did not patent the idea and he left that to Richardson in 1917. The submarine hydroplane was invented earlier so was not a Garrett invention as has been suggested elsewhere. Another of Garrett's achievements was his work on purifying air in confined spaces which lead to the development of his patented *Pneumatophore,* which was used in the *Resurgam* and in his later submarines. This device was the first closed circuit rebreather diving system that was successfully demonstrated, possibly pre-empting Henry A. Fleuss, who is usually credited with the invention.[74]

And yet the little boat still lies neglected on the seabed off Rhyl, some twenty years after she was accidentally found by a trawler; still largely intact, but damaged and not getting any better as the years go by. The *Resurgam* is unique and is the oldest surviving powered submarine so is worth saving for that reason alone. The Lamm-type power plant on board may be the last surviving example of its kind and the remains of the world's first diving rebreather may still be found inside her hull. No-one appears to own the *Resurgam* so she is the property of the Crown by default. George W. Garrett, grandson of Rev. George W. Garrett, transferred '*...any title to, or claim that we (the entire Garrett family) may have in the Resurgam to the Royal Navy Submarine Museum for the sum of one pound sterling*'[75] and the Receiver of Wreck could not find any valid claim of ownership.[76]

Resurgam was vulnerable when found in 1996 but since then the ravages of time and the elements have taken further toll. Ten years since she was first found still nothing had been done to save the submarine. So three eminent maritime archaeologists, James P. Delgado, Michael McCarthy and Robert S. Neyland took the unusual step of publishing an open letter in the International Journal of Nautical Archaeology. The letter was addressed to '*maritime archaeologists, shipwreck conservators, ICUCH/ICOMOS members, heritage practitioners, and stakeholders in Resurgam, about the endangered historic submarine Resurgam (1880)*'. In the letter the authors expressed:

'*great and growing concerns at the endangered status of one of the world's greatest submerged maritime heritage treasures, the* Resurgam'

The letter is reproduced in full in Appendix 2.[77]

Despite these efforts and *Resurgam's* unique status, time has moved on and some 20 years later still nothing has been done to protect this submarine! Given enough time

---

[74] Davis 1947 p194, Quick 1970
[75] Wessex 2007
[76] Robbins 1999
[77] Delgado et al, 2006

the heritage management 'problem' that is *Resurgam* will disappear because she will turn completely to rust, collapse, and wash away with the tide. This unique monument to Victorian engineering needs to be rescued and saved for posterity – so effective action needs to be taken before it is too late.

Appendix 1: Tables

Table 1 - AUSS Targets from 1996

Name	Latitude	Longitude	Notes
AUSS1	53° 23.722 N	003° 33.314 W	Resurgam hull (accuracy 20 m)
AUSS2	53° 23.682 N	003° 33.398 W	Large target
AUSS3	53° 23.747 N	003° 33.275 W	Significant target, some shadow
AUSS4	53° 23.667 N	003° 33.401 W	Significant target, some shadow
AUSS5	53° 23.658 N	003° 33.297 W	Significant target, some shadow
AUSS6	53° 23.686 N	003° 33.333 W	Minor target
AUSS7	53° 23.716 N	003° 33.344 W	Minor target
AUSS8	53° 23.702 N	003° 33.357 W	Minor target
AUSS9	53° 23.691 N	003° 33.348 W	Minor target
AUSS10	53° 23.688 N	003° 33.412 W	Minor target
AUSS11	53° 23.723 N	003° 33.407 W	Minor target

Table 2: ADU Targets 03 Jun 1997

CS001A	53° 23.734 N	003° 33.312 W
CS002	53° 23.730 N	003° 33.297 W
CS003	53° 23.733 N	003° 33.302 W
CS004	53° 23.737 N	003° 33.304 W
CS005	53° 23.778 N	003° 33.333 W
CS006	53° 23.779 N	003° 33.337 W
CS007	53° 23.740 N	003° 33.314 W
CS008	53° 23.727 N	003° 33.294 W
CS009	53° 23.730 N	003° 33.309 W
CS010	53° 23.729 N	003° 33.314 W
CS013	53° 23.747 N	003° 33.364 W

Table 3: Corner Co-ordinates

Corner	Latitude	Longitude
North-West	53° 23.753 N	003° 33.377 W
North-East	53° 23.754 N	003° 33.287 W
South-East	53° 23.670 N	003° 33.286 W
South-West	53° 23.699 N	003° 33.376 W

Table 4: Beacon positions

Beacon	Latitude	Longitude
A	53° 23.777 N	003° 33.276 W
B	53° 23.708 N	003° 33.261 W
C	53° 23.699 N	003° 33.386 W
D	53° 23.753 N	003° 33.412 W

Table 5: Control Point Positions

Point	Latitude	Longitude
Bow	53° 23.7269 N	003° 33.3361 W
B	53° 23.7262 N	003° 33.3403 W
SA	53° 23.7295 N	003° 33.3368 W
SB	53° 23.7305 N	003° 33.3304 W
SC	53° 23.7293 N	003° 33.3240 W
ST	53° 23.7340 N	003° 33.3295 W
S	53° 23.7263 N	003° 33.3209 W
PA	53° 23.7243 N	003° 33.3374 W

PB	53° 23.7240 N	003° 33.3305 W
PC	53° 23.7235 N	003° 33.3242 W
PT	53° 23.7221 N	003° 33.3289 W
STERN	53° 23.7265 N	003° 33.3252 W
ALEX_A	53° 23.7234 N	003° 33.3323 W
ALEX_C	53° 23.7220 N	003° 33.3308 W

Table 6: Metal detector targets

ID	Latitude	Longitude	Date Found	Found By	Notes
C001	53° 23.7223 N	003° 33.3296 W	04.06	ROV	STRAP_S, Strap
C003	53° 23.7228 N	003° 33.3310 W	04.06	ROV	STRAP_N, Strap
C005	53° 23.7243 N	003° 33.3313 W	10.06	Holt	Block, reburied
C006	53° 23.7242 N	003° 33.3280 W	10.06	Holt	Plate, RES-A006
C007	53° 23.7251 N	003° 33.3309 W	10.06	Holt	Unknown, deeply buried
C008	53° 23.7245 N	003° 33.3274 W	10.06	Holt	Unknown, deeply buried
C009	53° 23.7249 N	003° 33.3253 W	10.06	Holt	Very small frag, reburied
C010	53° 23.7253 N	003° 33.3253 W	10.06	Holt	Very small frag, reburied
C011	53° 23.7246 N	003° 33.3244 W	13.06	Williams	Unknown
C012	53° 23.7288 N	003° 33.3353 W	13.06	Adams	Unknown
C013	53° 23.7288 N	003° 33.3322 W	13.06	Adams	Unknown, PA
C014	53° 23.7159 N	003° 33.3396 W	12.06	Momber	Unknown, 20 m to south
C015	53° 23.7201 N	003° 33.3300 W	12.06	Momber	Unknown, 10 m to south

C016	53° 23.7247 N	003° 33.3278 W	12.06	Momber	Unknown, is C008?
C017	53° 23.7248 N	003° 33.3188 W	15.06	Holt	Unknown, 7 m to east
C018	53° 23.7286 N	003° 33.3292 W	11.06	Thomas	Unknown
C020	53° 23.7200 N	003° 33.3326 W	13.06	Jones	Unknown, 10 m to south

Table 7: Uri Geller Targets

UG1	53° 23.7276 N	003° 33.3264 W	Excavated, no target
UG2	53° 23.7270 N	003° 33.3256 W	Excavated, no target
UG3	53° 23.7264 N	003° 33.3178 W	Searched, no target

Appendix 2: The Open Letter

An Open Letter to maritime archaeologists, shipwreck conservators, ICUCH/ICOMOS members, heritage practitioners, and stakeholders in *Resurgam*, about the endangered historic submarine *Resurgam* (1880)

Dear Editor,

As overseas maritime archaeologists with professional experience in the assessment and management of historic submarines, and as practitioners aware of the individual and collective importance of these early submarines as archaeological sites, we are led to express our great and growing concerns at the endangered status of one of the world's greatest submerged maritime heritage treasures, the *Resurgam*.

Many in Britain will be aware of *Resurgam's* status as one of the most important early submarines, a product of a great engineering brain, a man operating and inventing years ahead of his time. Few maritime heritage practitioners worldwide are not aware of the significance of *Resurgam*. None will doubt its importance, all would attest to the need to have the ongoing damage that is occurring at the site immediately cease. Adverse newspaper reports regularly appear. Rarely do we not read of some accident or incident contributing to its accelerated degradation, or rendering it even more at risk by souvenir-hunting, unauthorised salvage, or flagrant vandalism. Rarely are there not calls for immediate action from concerned Britons. The inability of local authorities to agree on the best means of physically protecting this world recognised ground-breaking submarine-boat is rendered the more remarkable at a distance, given that its preservation can be so easily and economically effected without the need to resolve issues regarding ownership and responsibility.

All that is required presently, notwithstanding the well-known competing claims and duties, is to move the vessel to a more benign (less saline, calmer and safer) underwater environment. By this means in-situ conservation will have begun, and unauthorised access been prevented. Then, with the submarine in a secure and slowly-stabilising state, due consideration could be given to enhancing its status. The attachment of anodes (a proven initiative) and monitored technical and recreational/tourism visitations are two minimum cost initiatives which could be considered. All other issues could then be resolved in an appropriate manner and to the satisfaction of the stakeholders.

We understand that there are highly capable and experienced archaeologists, conservators and salvage operators in Britain and in nearby European countries, who are willing to combine and help save *Resurgam*, in the manner outlined above. To that end we urge those officials in Britain and Wales capable of decision-making in respect of *Resurgam* to act quickly and effectively and to harness their largesse, expertise and commitment on behalf of what we perceive is an unnecessarily endangered maritime heritage site of global significance.

James P. Delgado
Director, Vancouver Maritime Museum
Michael McCarthy
Western Australian Maritime Museum
Robert S. Neyland
Underwater Archaeology Branch, US Naval Historical Center

The International Journal of Nautical Archaeology (2006) 35.1: 145

References

3H Consulting, 2016, 3D Trilateration, available at http://www.3hconsulting.com/techniques/Tech3DTrilatDSM.html

Admiralty, 1878, Digest No. 56-59, 'Rev. GW Garrett's submarine torpedo boat', 20 Dec 1878, National Archives, ADM 12/1060

Admiralty, 1880, Digest No. 59/5-67, 'Submarine inventions by Revd GW Garrett', 8 April 1880, digest 59-8, National Archives, ADM 12/1023

Archaeological Diving Unit (ADU), 1996, unpublished site report 96/03

Archaeological Diving Unit (ADU), 1997, SubMap Project Design, unpublished

Archaeological Diving Unit (ADU), 1999, unpublished site report 99/07

Bacon R., 1940, *From 1900 Onward*, Hutchinson & Co., London

Barber F.M., 1875, *Lecture on Submarine Boats and Their Application to Torpedo Operations*, US Torpedo Station, Newport RI

BBC, 2012, Chester divers attempt to save Resurgam II submarine, 6 Aug., available at http://www.bbc.co.uk/news/uk-england-19146040

Bowers, P., 1999, *the Garrett Enigma and the Early Submarine Pioneers*, Airlife Publishing Ltd., Shrewsbury, ISBN 1 84037 066 1

Bowyer M., 2000, Resurgam 1999 Report, in Nautical Archaeology Society Newsletter 2000:1, p9

Burcher R. & Rydill L., 1994, Concepts in Submarine Design, Cambridge University Press, ISBN 0 5215 5926 X

Campbell T., 2000, *The CSS H.L. Hunley, Confederate Submarine*, Burd Street Press, ISBN 1 57249 175 2

Cochran Boilers Ltd., 1998, Cochran 100 Years in Boiler Making, Cochran Boilers Ltd.

Compton-Hall R., 1999, *The Submarine Pioneers*, Sutton Publishing Ltd., ISBN 0 7509 2154 4

Dash M., 1990, British Submarine Policy 1853-1918, Unpublished PhD thesis, University of London, http://www.docstoc.com/docs/51440452/British-Submarine-Policy-1853-1918, Accessed Dec 2014

Davis R.H., 1947, *Breathing in Irrespirable Atmospheres*, Siebe Gorman & Co. Ltd, London

Davis R.H., 1955, *Deep Diving and Submarine Operations*, Sixth Edition, Siebe Gorman and Co. Ltd.

Dean, M., 1998, The Submarine Boat *Resurgam,* in *Maritime Heritage* 2.2 33-35

Dean, Hildred, Holt, Lawrence, Lawrence, Liscoe and Oxley, 2007, *Resurgam* - a Lesson to Us All, unpublished paper

Delgado J. et al, 2006, An Open Letter to maritime archaeologists, shipwreck conservators, ICUCH/ICOMOS members, heritage practitioners, and stakeholders in Resurgam, about the endangered historic submarine Resurgam (1880), International Journal of Nautical Archaeology 35:1, p145

Essex Standard, 1878, Reporting on Cassell's Family Magazine, 09 November

Fish J., 1996, Letter to Bill Garrett, Resurgam Search Targets Located, 8th July

Gardiner R. (Ed.), 1992, *Steam, Steel & Shellfire: The Steam Warship 1815 - 1905*, Conway Maritime Press, ISBN 0 85177 564 0

Garrett, G.W., 1878, *Submarine Boats for Placing Torpedoes &c.*, The Commissioners of Patents Sale Department, London

Garrett G., 1879, Letter to Cochran & Co., 31st March, Royal Navy Submarine Museum A1989/171

Gorton M, 1989, Search for the Resurgam, Diver Magazine, November

Gorton M., 1996a, How I Found the Resurgam, Diver Magazine, April

Gorton M., 1996b, What a Piece of Work, Diver Magazine, April

Graphic, 1880, The Garrett Submarine Torpedo Boat, Graphic magazine, 17 January 1880

Gray E., 1975, *The Devil's Device*, Seeley, Service & Co. Ltd., London, ISBN 0 85422 104 2

Gregory D., 2000, In-situ corrosion studies on the submarine Resurgam - A preliminary assessment of her state of preservation, Conservation and Management of Archaeological Sites, volume 4, p93-100

Hildred A., 1997a, SubMap daily log, unpublished

Hildred A., 1997b, 1:1 finds drawings on polythene, unpublished

Hildred A., Holt P. & Boston N., 1997, Report to the Committee on Historic Wreck, Resurgam Excavation and Site Survey 1997

Hiscock, K, ed. 1996. Marine Nature Conservation Review: Rationale and Methods. Peterborough, Joint Nature Conservation Committee, Coasts and Seas of the United Kingdom, MNCR series

History of Wallasey, 2016, The Story of the Shipyards of Old Seacombe, available at http://www.historyofwallasey.co.uk

Holt P., 1997, SubMap Project Outline Site Survey Plan, Sonardyne International Ltd.

Holt P. & Hildred A., 1999, SubMap Project Site Survey Report, SubMap Project

Holt P., 1999, Resurgam Revisited, in Nautical Archaeology Society Newsletter 2009

Holt P., 2015, *HM Submarine A7, An Archaeological Assessment*, British Archaeological Reports British Series no. 613, Oxford, ISBN 978 1407 31374 0

Holt R., 1997, Biological survey of the wreck of the Resurgam, Joint Nature Conservation Council for the SubMap Project

Hool J. & Nutter K, 2003, *Damned Un-English Machines*, Tempus Publishing Ltd., ISBN 0 7524 2781 4

Lamm E., 1872, *Improvement in supplying Steam to Travelling Engines.* United States of America, Patent No. 129969

Liverpool Echo, 1925, The Voyage of the First Submarine, 8 December

Liverpool Mercury, 1878, Wednesday 07 August, New Submarine Vessel

London Daily News, 1880, Weather reports 23-27 February

Long E.S., 2011, Resurgam Part 1, Liverpool Nautical Research Society Bulletin, Volume 55, No. 4, March 2012

Long E.S., 2011, Resurgam Part 2, Liverpool Nautical Research Society Bulletin, Volume 56, No. 1, June 2012

Manchester Courier and Lancashire General Advertiser, 1879a, New Garrett Submarine Torpedo Boat, 28 November

Manchester Courier and Lancashire General Advertiser, 1879b, New Garrett Submarine Torpedo Boat, 06 December

Manchester Courier and Lancashire General Advertiser, 1880a, The Garrett Submarine Torpedo Boat "Resurgam", 03 January

Manchester Courier and Lancashire General Advertiser, 1880b, The Garrett Submarine Torpedo Boat, 08 May

Manchester Evening News, 2007, Divers Take the Plunge, 15 October

Marine Engineer, 1880a, The Great Submarine Boat, 01 January

Marine Engineer, 1880b, Editorial Notes, 01 March

Molecular Products, 2009, A Guide to Breathing Rates in Confined Environments, Molecular Products, available at http://www.molecularproducts.com/technical-library.htm

Morris R. K., 1998, *John P. Holland, 1841-1914: Inventor of the Modern Submarine*, University of South Carolina Press, ISBN 1 57003 236 X

Murphy, W. S., 1987, *Father of the Submarine: The Life of the Reverend George Garrett Pasha*, William Kimber & Co. Ltd., London, ISBN 0 7183 0654 6

Newell M., 1996, The Resurgam Pre-Disturbance and Recovery: Preliminary Research Design and Methodology, Georgia Archaeological Institute

Oil & Gas Journal, 1995, Liverpool Bay piggybacked gas pipeline installed with bottom tow, 25 Dec.

Osiris Projects, 2011, Multibeam sonar survey data, unpublished

Ostler W., 1915, *Science and War*; an address delivered at the University of Leeds medical school on October 1, Oxford University Press, London

Pesce G.L., 1906, *La Navigation Sous-Marin*, Vuibert & Nony, Paris

Quick D. 1970, *A History of Closed Circuit Oxygen Underwater Breathing Apparatus*, School of Underwater Medicine, HMAS Penguin, Project 1/70

Rhyl Advertiser, 1880, First Trial Trip of the Garrett Submarine Torpedo Boat the Resurgam, December 20

Rhyl Journal, 1880, 28 February

Rhyl Journal, 1925, Ship That Never Returned, November 28

Richardson, 1917, Improvements in or relating to Submarine or Submersible Boats, Patent GB106330 (A)

RNSM, 1879, Garrett and Cochran & Co. documents, Royal Navy Submarine Museum A2007/349

Robbins V., 1999, In Minutes and Results of the *Resurgam* Meeting Held on 18/2/99 at the Mary Rose Trust, unpublished minutes

Sennett R. & Oram H., 1908, *The Marine Steam Engine*, Longmans Green and Co., Ninth Edition

Stewart M., 2004, *Monturiol's Dream: The Extraordinary Story of the Submarine Inventor Who Wanted to Save the World*, Pantheon Books, ISBN 978-0375414398

SubMap, 1997, Dive logs from the NAS volunteers, unpublished

SubMap, 1997, Dive logs from the survey team on *Terschelling*, unpublished

Sueter M, 1907, *The Evolution of the Submarine Boat, Mine and Torpedo*, J. Griffin & Co., Portsmouth

The Engineer, 1875, Fireless locomotives, May 7, p307

The Engineer, 1882, Garrett's Submarine Torpedo Boat, January 6, p8 & p13

The Engineer, 1901, Submarine Boats No. II, Feb 8, p146

University College of North Wales, 1981, The Resurgam Project, University College of North Wales, Bangor

Wareing S., 2012, Resurgam, a Historical and Archaeological Analysis, MA Maritime Archaeology & History dissertation, University of Bristol

Wessex Archaeology, 2007, Resurgam Designated Site Assessment, 53111.03ss

Wignall S., 1978, The Quest for Gt. Britain's first submersible the ' Resurgam', Maritime Wales No. 3 March 1978, ISSN 0308 2334

Wilson A.K., 1900, Submarine Boats Considered by USA House Committee, 3 August 1900, National Archives ADM 1/7462

Wilson A.K., 1901, Submarine boats, 21 January 1901, National Archives ADM 1/7515